T0215841

Lecture Notes in Computer Science 10830

Commenced Publication in 1973
Founding and Former Series Editors:
Gerhard Goos, Juris Hartmanis, and Jan van Leeuwen

More information about this series at http://www.springer.com/series/8183

Marina L. Gavrilova · C. J. Kenneth Tan
Alexei Sourin (Eds.)

Transactions on Computational Science XXXII

Special Issue on Cybersecurity and Biometrics

 Springer

Editors-in-Chief

Marina L. Gavrilova
University of Calgary
Calgary, AB
Canada

C. J. Kenneth Tan
Sardina Systems OÜ
Tallinn
Estonia

Guest Editor

Alexei Sourin
Nanyang Technological University
Singapore
Singapore

ISSN 0302-9743   ISSN 1611-3349   (electronic)
Lecture Notes in Computer Science
ISSN 1866-4733   ISSN 1866-4741   (electronic)
Transactions on Computational Science
ISBN 978-3-662-56671-8   ISBN 978-3-662-56672-5   (eBook)
https://doi.org/10.1007/978-3-662-56672-5

Library of Congress Control Number: 2018936192

This Springer imprint is published by the registered company Springer-Verlag GmbH, DE
part of Springer Nature
The registered company address is: Heidelberger Platz 3, 14197 Berlin, Germany

LNCS Transactions on Computational Science

Computational science, an emerging and increasingly vital field, is now widely recognized as an integral part of scientific and technical investigations, affecting researchers and practitioners in areas ranging from aerospace and automotive research to biochemistry, electronics, geosciences, mathematics, and physics. Computer systems research and the exploitation of applied research naturally complement each other. The increased complexity of many challenges in computational science demands the use of supercomputing, parallel processing, sophisticated algorithms, and advanced system software and architecture. It is therefore invaluable to have input by systems research experts in applied computational science research.

Transactions on Computational Science focuses on original high-quality research in the realm of computational science in parallel and distributed environments, also encompassing the underlying theoretical foundations and the applications of large-scale computation.

The journal offers practitioners and researchers the opportunity to share computational techniques and solutions in this area, to identify new issues, and to shape future directions for research, and it enables industrial users to apply leading-edge, large-scale, high-performance computational methods.

In addition to addressing various research and application issues, the journal aims to present material that is validated – crucial to the application and advancement of the research conducted in academic and industrial settings. In this spirit, the journal focuses on publications that present results and computational techniques that are verifiable.

Scope

The scope of the journal includes, but is not limited to, the following computational methods and applications:

- Aeronautics and Aerospace
- Astrophysics
- Big Data Analytics
- Bioinformatics
- Biometric Technologies
- Climate and Weather Modeling
- Communication and Data Networks
- Compilers and Operating Systems
- Computer Graphics
- Computational Biology
- Computational Chemistry
- Computational Finance and Econometrics

- Computational Fluid Dynamics
- Computational Geometry
- Computational Number Theory
- Data Representation and Storage
- Data Mining and Data Warehousing
- Information and Online Security
- Grid Computing
- Hardware/Software Co-design
- High-Performance Computing
- Image and Video Processing
- Information Systems
- Information Retrieval
- Modeling and Simulations
- Mobile Computing
- Numerical and Scientific Computing
- Parallel and Distributed Computing
- Robotics and Navigation
- Supercomputing
- System-on-Chip Design and Engineering
- Virtual Reality and Cyberworlds
- Visualization

Editorial

The *Transactions on Computational Science* journal is published as part of the Springer series *Lecture Notes in Computer Science*, and is devoted to a range of computational science issues, from theoretical aspects to application-dependent studies and the validation of emerging technologies.

The journal focuses on original high-quality research in the realm of computational science in parallel and distributed environments, encompassing the facilitating theoretical foundations and the applications of large-scale computations and massive data processing. Practitioners and researchers share computational techniques and solutions in the area, identify new issues, and shape future directions for research, as well as enable industrial users to apply the techniques presented.

The current issue is devoted to research on *Cybersecurity and Biometrics* and is edited by Alexei Sourin, Professor, Nanyang Technological University, Singapore. This special issue includes eight articles preceded by the guest editor's preface. These articles were selected following the 2016 International Conference on Cyberworlds, held in Chongqing, China. The authors of the selected papers are from Europe, North America, and Asia.

We would like to extend our sincere appreciation to the special issue guest editor Alexei Sourin, for his relentless work, diligence, and vision in preparing this special issue on a very relevant and important topic. We would also like to thank all of the authors for submitting their papers to the special issue and the associate editors and referees for their valuable work. We would like to express our gratitude to the LNCS editorial staff of Springer, who supported us at every stage of the project.

We do hope that the fine collection of papers presented in this special issue will be a valuable resource for *Transactions on Computational Science* readers and will stimulate further research in the vibrant area of computational science applications.

February 2018

Marina L. Gavrilova
C. J. Kenneth Tan

Guest Editor's Preface

Cyberworlds are information spaces and communities that use computer technologies to augment the way we interact, participate in business, and receive information throughout the world. Cyberworlds have an ever-growing impact on our lives and on the evolution of the world economy. Examples include social networking services, 3D shared virtual communities, and massively multiplayer online role-playing games. The 2017 International Conference on Cyberworlds was hosted by the University of Chester, UK, during September 20–22, 2017, with a particular interest in the areas of virtual and augmented reality and cybersecurity. This issue of the journal presents eight select extended and improved conference papers.

The first article, "Investigating Multimodal Warnings for Distracted Smartphone Users on the Move in Potentially Dangerous Situations," considers distractions which can be caused by smart devices in our everyday life. The authors put the needs of the user into focus and investigate the acceptance, potential dangers, and events to be warned about, as well as types of warning, reaction time and legal regulations.

The second article, "EEG-based Mental Workload and Stress Monitoring of Crew Members in Maritime Virtual Simulator," proposes a novel mental workload recognition algorithm and describes its successful application to monitoring brain states of crew members in a maritime simulator. The authors argue that EEG can be a promising evaluation tool applicable in human factors study for the maritime domain.

The issue continues by the third article titled "An Approach for Detecting Web Defacement with Self-Healing Capabilities," which proposes a Web defacement and intrusion monitoring tool that could be a possible solution for the rapid identification of altered or deleted Web pages. The authors claim that the proposed tool may be used for intrusion detection as well for regeneration of the original content of a website after the website has been defaced.

The cybersecurity topic is continued by the fourth article, "Assessing Opinions on Software as a Weapon in the Context of (Inter)national Security." The authors argue that modern life is permeated by software which provides a large attack surface, ranging from generic, low-impact malware attacks, to sophistically created and targeted code touted as a next generation of weapons. The authors analyze the results of the questionnaire conducted on the attitudes toward using software as a weapon.

The fifth article, "OpenGL|D — An Alternative Approach to Multi-user Architecture," introduces a novel distributed architecture with the focus on multiplayer games. The authors specifically address the scalability and real-time performance of concurrent synchronization designs as a core of all multi-user applications.

The authors of "Image Quality-Based Illumination-Invariant Face Recognition" propose an adaptive discrete wavelet transform-based face recognition approach, which, as they argue, will normalize the illumination distortion using quality-based normalization approaches. The presented experimental results show that the proposed method outperforms some well-known face recognition approaches.

The seventh article "Synthesizing Imagined Faces Based on Relevance Feedback" describes the development of a user-friendly system that can create a facial image from a corresponding image in the user's mind. The experimental results presented by the authors show that the proposed technique succeeded in generating mental images of Asian faces.

Finally, the eighth article, "Neurofeedback Training for Enhancement of the Focused Attention Related to Athletic Performance in Elite Rifle Shooters," studies how to optimize the focused attention of expert rifle shooters with the use of neuro-feedback training tools as well as how to enhance their shooting performance. The authors designed, implemented, and conducted an experiment and confirmed that the proposed tools can boost the performance of the shooters.

The organizers of the conference are very grateful to Professor Marina Gavrilova, Editor-in-Chief of the *Transactions on Computational Science*, for the continuing support and assistance. We also wish to thank the authors for their high-quality contributions, as well as the reviewers for their invaluable advice, which helped to improve the papers.

January 2018   Alexei Sourin

LNCS Transactions on Computational Science – Editorial Board

Contents

Investigating Multimodal Warnings for Distracted Smartphone Users
on the Move in Potentially Dangerous Situations 1
    Melinda C. Braun, Sandra Beuck, Matthias Wölfel,
    and Alexander Scheurer

EEG-Based Mental Workload and Stress Monitoring of Crew Members
in Maritime Virtual Simulator................................ 15
    Wei Lun Lim, Yisi Liu, Salem Chandrasekaran Harihara Subramaniam,
    Serene Hui Ping Liew, Gopala Krishnan, Olga Sourina,
    Dimitrios Konovessis, Hock Eng Ang, and Lipo Wang

An Approach for Detecting Web Defacement
with Self-healing Capabilities................................ 29
    Mfundo Masango, Francois Mouton, Palesa Antony,
    and Bokang Mangoale

Assessing Opinions on Software as a Weapon in the Context
of (Inter)national Security.................................. 43
    Jantje A. M. Silomon and Mark Patrick Roeling

OpenGL|D - An Alternative Approach to Multi-user Architecture 57
    Karsten Pedersen, Christos Gatzidis, and Wen Tang

Image Quality-Based Illumination-Invariant Face Recognition............ 75
    Fatema Tuz Zohra and Marina Gavrilova

Synthesizing Imagined Faces Based on Relevance Feedback............. 90
    Caie Xu, Shota Fushimi, Masahiro Toyoura, Jiayi Xu,
    and Xiaoyang Mao

NeuroFeedback Training for Enhancement of the Focused Attention
Related to Athletic Performance in Elite Rifle Shooters 106
    Yisi Liu, Salem Chandrasekaran Harihara Subramaniam,
    Olga Sourina, Eesha Shah, Joshua Chua, and Kirill Ivanov

Author Index 121

Investigating Multimodal Warnings for Distracted Smartphone Users on the Move in Potentially Dangerous Situations

Melinda C. Braun, Sandra Beuck, Matthias Wölfel$^{(\boxtimes)}$, and Alexander Scheurer

Furtwangen University, Furtwangen im Schwarzwald, Germany
{braunmel,beus,woma,salx}@hs-furtwangen.de

Abstract. The use of smart devices has become an integrated part of our everyday life. Communication is now possible any place and any time. The distraction caused by these devices, however, can lead to potentially dangerous situations. To mitigate these situations, various researchers have proposed and developed solutions to analyze the environment and to alert the user if a situation is evaluated dangerous. While seeking technical solutions, the concerns of the users are usually not addressed. With our studies we put the needs of the user into focus and investigated the acceptance, potential dangers, events to be warned about, type of warning, reaction time and legal regulations.

Keywords: Distracted pedestrians · Smartphone usage
Safety applications · User acceptance · Warning modalities

1 Introduction

The use of smart devices has become an integrated part of our everyday life. Communication is now possible anywhere and any time. The distraction by these devices, however, can lead to potentially dangerous situations. The word *selfie* has already entered general parlance. It stands for photos that people make of themselves, with their smartphone. A statistic from *priceonomics* [1] shows that since 2014, at least 49 people have died while making a selfie. The most common causes of death were falling from heights, drowning and being hit by train. These shocking numbers demonstrate the carelessness of smartphone users by risking their own lives and possibly the lives of others. Since distracted users—not only taking photos but reading, typing, gaming while walking—are becoming increasingly harmful to themselves and others, some countries already have reacted by regulating smartphones usage in public places. For instance Honolulu became the first major US city to reduce injuries and deaths caused by *distracted walking* by introducing fines up to \$ 99 for crossing streets while using smartphones [2].

As an interesting alternative to regulations by governments, researches try to find technical solutions (see Sect. 2): Their idea is to analyze the environment

© Springer-Verlag GmbH Germany, part of Springer Nature 2018
M. L. Gavrilova et al. (Eds.): Trans. on Comput. Sci. XXXII, LNCS 10830, pp. 1–14, 2018.
https://doi.org/10.1007/978-3-662-56672-5_1

by divers sensors and to alert the user if a situation is potentially dangerous. While such systems seem to be useful at first sight and might indeed lead to a reduction in accidents, it is an nearly untouched question whether the use of such applications would be accepted by the users. A first attempt into this direction has been addressed in a paper by some of the authors of this publication [3]. While the paper was focused more on the willingness of distracted smartphone users to be interrupted in potentially dangerous situations this publication focus more on the presentation of warnings, events to be warned about and type of warning.

2   Previous Work

This section reviews previous work on user behavior and type of warnings. The reader interested in technical solutions are referred to *HeadsUp* by Zhou [4], *InfraSee* [5], *UltraSee* [6] and *CrashAlert* [7]. They all have in common that all use additional sensors, not yet integrated into the smartphone, for instance, depth cameras to recognize upcoming obstacles. This is a technical challenge which still needs to be solved to be able to provide reliable alert systems.

2.1   User Behavior

The behavior of mobile phone and smartphone users have been analyzed in a few of publications of which we can review only a small portion here. The paper by Pizzamiglioa *et al.* [8] measures the different levels of distraction encountered by pedestrians while walking using accelerometers for movement and mobile EEG for electroencephalogram signals from the brain. A study focusing on injuries caused by mobile phone usage has been conducted by Nasar and Troyer [9]. They analyzed the contents of the *National Electronic Injury Surveillance Systems*-Database (NEISS) [10], which is a database that records information about injuries from 100 American hospitals categorized by the involvement of consumer products. They could confirm that an increasing number of pedestrian injuries, between 2004 and 2010, are caused by mobile phone usage in public spaces.

Since more accidents seem to happen due to heedless usage of smartphones the question arise if users are aware of the potential dangers. The user's perspective is shown by a study released by the *American Academy of Orthopedic Surgeons* about distracted walking [11]. 2,000 adults were asked about their smartphone habits, specifically about distracted walking, distracted walking incidents and how often they observe this in others. 28% agreed to use their mobile device at least sometimes while walking, and 26% have already experienced a distracted walking incident. They define a distracted walking incident as at least bumping into something or somebody. 84% have *observed* distracted walking (at least sometimes). As shown here, there is a big difference between self-awareness and foreign perception. This may mean that users know the dangers, but assume no risk for themselves. To investigate what application is more distracting Haga *et al.* [12] compared smartphone usage with the task of texting, watching a video and playing a game. Their participants had to walk a $3 \times 3\,$m perimeter with a straight line to walk on. They measured how accurately they step on the line, as well as how timely they react to visual and auditory cues around them. They found that playing a game was the most distracting usage, followed by texting.

2.2   Modality and Specificity of Warnings

The way different warning have to be presented has been widely ignored in the papers providing technical solutions. One exception is the paper by Hincapié-Ramos and Irani [7] which includes a brief evaluation of user's preferences of warnings types: it analyzed different methods of displaying a small slice of the device camera's image on the user's screen while walking. Thus, the user does not need to move their head up to see upcoming static or dynamic obstacles. The authors used three different forms of displaying the camera's image: *color image* shows a slice of the camera's image, *depth image* is a visualization of depth for a fixed distance of 5 m, and *masked image* combines both, showing the user the closest obstacles by abstracting the image with a mask. All display methods presented a red alert when the obstacle was less than 2 m away. The study showed that the participants found the colored and masked images more detailed but also a lot harder to recognize compared to the depth images, thus they needing more attention to the former.

There are various studies and standards on visual, auditory and multimodal warning types (auditory and visual in combination) in other context. Each modality has different advantages and disadvantages:

Visual Warnings

For instance in the area of visual warnings there are the possibilities to warn by colors, shapes or text (DIN ISO 3864-1 2012-06 [13]; DIN ISO 3864-3 2012-11 [14]; ANSI Z535.4-2007 [15]) and address the human sense of sight [16]. A good possibility for this are icons, since these are a visual simplification of complex processes and the people are increasingly getting used to their meanings and existence by current developments [17]. Icons can either be abstract or represent objects of the real world. If they do not, their meaning must first be learned by the recipient. In addition to pictorial representations, it is possible to use textual descriptions. However, this can be counterproductive or misleading in certain dangerous situations, for example when driving, since the reading takes too long and can slow down response times [17]. The German Institute for Standardization (DIN) has issued various standards for the representation of safety marks, colors and shapes. For warnings, it is recommended to use the geometric shape of a triangle in combination with yellow. Additional information, which can be represented graphically or textually can be placed at any position around the actual warning.

Auditive Warnings

Auditive warnings can be, for example abstract sounds such as sirens, bells or buzzer. These types of warnings need to be learned first and are easy to confuse, so they may not be appropriate for emergencies [18]. Another approach of auditory warnings are "auditory icons", which represent the natural sounds of everyday situations and therefore do not have to be learned. They can convey information about events and dangers through their meaning and are therefore potentially better understood than abstract sounds [19].

Multimodal Warnings

Visual and auditory warnings can also be combined as multimodal warnings. They can also be augmented with tactile feedback. According to Gaver [20], the use of both senses, the sense of sight and hearing, can increase the range of possible information and thus the intelligibility of the warning, since hearing and seeing are complementary forms of information processing.

3   Test Setup

The aim of our research is to find out users' preferences for warning systems on smartphones, investigate different warning modalities and evaluate participants reaction time according to the represented warning modalities. To test the participants within potentially dangerous real-life situations (events) without endangering them, we carefully designed an obstacle course in a fully protected and controlled environment on campus. To protocol the material for later analysis we filmed the participants, recorded the gaze (*Tobii Pro Glasses 2*) where possible to measure objective reaction times, logged events and asked the participants to fill out a questionnaire after walking the obstacle course.

3.1   Test Application

We decided to use a game because according to Haga *et al.* [12] it causes the strongest distraction for walking smartphone users and it is easier to control the overall experience of the participant. To create an ongoing and controlled level of distraction, remotely triggering warnings and to capturing data it was necessary to develop our own application consisting of a *game* played by the study participants and a *remote-control* used by a study assistant [3].

The game is a simple balancing exercise, the task is to keep a red ball in the middle of the screen. The optimal position is indicated by a circled gradient in the background of the game, as well as a visible score. Because the participants could simply hold the phone steady to balance the ball it was necessary to add random impulses in random directions that must be actively compensated for in order to attain a decent score and keep the participants' attention. If the ball touches the sides, points are deducted which is accompanied by a red flashing border. The random impulses combined with the point deduction urges the participant to focus their attention on the game and thus creates a constant level of distraction.

If the game receives the command to show a warning, a warning is presented as in. A tap on the screen hides the warning message again. The warning itself

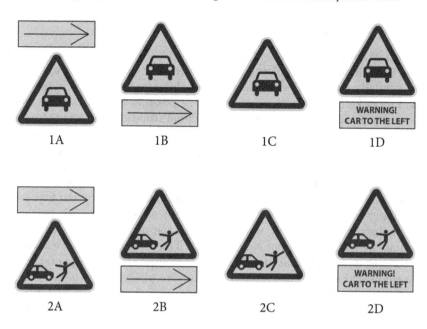

Fig. 1. Different combinations of the event "car from the left". Group 1 shows the non-specific warnings. In this context, unspecific means that the icon of the car itself informs the user about the nature of the danger, but not about where the car comes from and what kind of danger threatens the user himself. Group 2 shows the specific warnings which convey information about the position of the hazard and the possible consequences by the representation of the car in combination with the representation of a person. In addition to the icon, the direction of movement of the danger is transmitted. There are ways to inform the users either by arrows or by text, from which direction the danger is coming.

was designed to be understood quickly by using short and direct wording and a visualization that users associate with a warning by form and color, based on international traffic signs as demonstrated in the Fig. 1. The written words and the pictogram are necessary since the participants are not told about the true nature of the test. The game logs the current score every second, as well as any message or command it receives from the remote control.

3.2   Wizard of Oz Experiment

We examined the topic from the user's perspective and wanted to determine whether they would use a supportive system at all. Thus we see our investigations as an extension and basis for the technical development of supportive systems. From the user's point of view, a functioning system is sufficient. Therefore we decided to simulate this behavior by a *Wizard of Oz* experiment. The events are triggered by an unseen operator and lead the participants to believe that the computer system is acting autonomously. Every command produces a log entry on the game application.

3.3   Obstacle Course

The length of the route was about 400 m and it took each participant between three to five minutes to complete it. Four different events were set up to simulate potentially dangerous situations. The pathway as well as the events were designed to make these situations as natural as possible and to resemble everyday scenarios. To cover a broad variety of potential situations the events featured different aspects and characteristics: fast (bike), slow (pedestrian, car) or static obstacles (boxes) and loud (car) as well as quiet (bike, pedestrian, boxes).

The first two events on the way to the turning point were a cyclist and a pedestrian, trying to collide with the participant. They switched their positions after every participant to eliminate a possible bias introduced by the first event (by familiarity with the first warning). The actor assigned for each particular event was instructed to almost walk/drive into the participant but to avoid a collision at the last possible but safe moment. The third and fourth events had fixed positions and where placed on the way back from the turning point. Event three introduced boxes on the ground, which were placed after the participant passed for the first time. The fourth event was a car backing out of a parking space into the path the participant would take, but stopping well before he would pass behind it.

3.4   Terminal-Based Test

In order to test a broad variety of warnings in addition to the warnings given in the obstacle course we designed a terminal-based test. In the terminal-based test persons wearing headphones were shown various grades of specific (more detailed icons) and unspecific visual warnings (less detailed icons) as auditory warnings with information about the position of a hazard to which they had to respond. By comparing the results between the obstacle course and the terminal we can also indicate if the results from the field test can be transferred to a computer based test.

3.5   Safety Measures

The study was designed so that no participant was ever really exposed to a dangerous situation by taking part in this test. Every member of the test-team was instructed to be vigilant of the situation and to intervene when a real possible danger event occurred, i.e. any situation which was not part of our test (like other cars). All team members were remitted to avoid touching the participant, let alone causing a collision with them.

3.6   Study Groups

We focused our study mostly on young adults, since research shows that they are the demographic group with the highest risk [21]. In total, 96 randomly chosen

Table 1. Overview of user groups and distributions.

	Warning	No warning	Modality	Control	Sum
Female	8	12	6	6	32
Male	15	12	23	14	64
Total	23	24	29	20	96

participants took part in our study. A detailed overview is provided in Table 1. All participants personally owned a smartphone and were used to handling it.

Participants were separated into three main groups walk through the obstacle course while playing the game and one control group:

- *Warning*: While walking this group got warnings of upcoming obstacles.
- *No Warning*: While walking this group got *no* warnings of upcoming obstacles.
- *Modality*: While walking this group got different warning modalities and absolved an computer-based reaction test afterward.
- *Control*: This group were asked to answer a questionnaire only without walking or playing.

After the obstacle route, the participants were asked to answer a questionnaire. It was set up using mostly a 4-point *Likert Scale*. Strongly agree (4), agree (3), disagree (2) or strongly disagree (1). Additionally, there were multiple choice and free text questions.

4   Results

In this Section we present and discuss the results from the test with the different user groups. Please note that the results are dependent on the user group and experiment. Thus, not all groups are represented in any of the presented results.

4.1   Acceptance

Table 2 summarizes the answers to the question: *Would you consider installing an app to warn you of upcoming dangerous situations?*, which in the following we classify as *acceptance*. The participants statements on this question show a general attitude towards the use of safety applications. The average score of 2.6 states that approximately half of the participants would install and use such an application. This is particularly surprising since nearly all the participants (3.7) agreed that it could be dangerous to use a smartphone while walking.

Comparing the acceptance in the three groups it is immediately apparent that the group of participants with warnings had somewhat better values (2.8) than to the two other groups (*No Warning* (2.4) and *Control* (2.4)). The similarity of the latter two (p-value 0.8642) demonstrates that our test setup did not influence the attitude towards a safety system for smartphones. Using Wilcoxon

Table 2. Acceptance of the applications (standard deviations in brackets).

	Warning	NoWarning	Control	Sum
Female	3.1 (1.3)	2.4 (1.2)	2.7 (0.8)	2.7 (1.2)
Male	2.6 (0.8)	2.4 (1.3)	2.4 (1.2)	2.5 (1.1)
Total	2.9 (1.0)	2.4 (1.3)	2.5 (1.1)	2.6 (1.1)

Rank-Sum Test's interpretation, between the *Warning*-group and the other two groups, p-value ≈ 0.3, the differences can be rated as *small*. In absolute numbers, however, this means an increase of approximately 10% from 46% for those not experiencing the warnings compared to 56% for those who did. The participants group *Modality* had 55% since all members of this group got warnings this also supports the statement.

4.2   Potential Dangers

We asked participants for potentially dangerous conditions they wanted to be warned about: life-threatening situations (3.9) had the highest values followed by dangerous situations (3.7), possibly dangerous situations (3.1), dangerous areas (e.g. high traffic) (3.1), and dangerous times (e.g. rush hour) (2.6). These values show the participants' attitude towards different forms of risk management. They don't want to receive general warnings, the warnings need to be exactly classified. Especially the term *possibly dangerous situations* caused the participants to accept the warning form than an explicit warning such as *dangerous areas*, although a *possibly dangerous situation* could be more relevant regarding the hazard level. As the high rating for dangerous times shows, users prefer time relevant and explicit notifications in their individual situations not for *dangerous times* in general.

4.3   Events to Be Warned About

According to the participants subjective assessment, cars and cyclists are the most dangerous events (93% cars, 62% cyclists). 31% of the subjects, however, do not want to be warned about cars, which shows that while they recognize that the situation can be dangerous, they still do not want to be warned. Only 10% of the subjects consider pedestrians dangerous. 34% say they do not want to be warned about pedestrians. To consider a car as the most dangerous obstacle seems to be quite logical from the user's perspective, since cars are fast and powerful and already known as dangerous for pedestrians unlike other pedestrians who usually are weaker and slower. The question is why do participants classify cars to be dangerous and decide not to be warned nevertheless. A reason for that could be the difference between self-perception and perception of others. In this case users do not assume that cars are dangerous to them, but they might be for others.

Table 3. Type of warning.

	Tactile	Acoustic	Visual			
			Pop-Up	Overlay	Brightness	Turning black
Activate	75%	51%	36%	22%	9%	10%
Deactivate	16%	31%	33%	30%	42%	66%
Difference	58%	19%	3%	−7%	−33%	−55%

4.4   Type of Warning

The participant's use or acceptance of safety applications strongly depends on the type of warning. Table 3 summarizes the type of notification the users would activate or deactivate. We found that the results didn't change much over the three investigated groups and thus did not present them separately. While 75% would activate *tactile* (vibration) warnings, only 51% of the participant would activate *acoustic* warnings. Surprisingly all types of *visual* warnings would not be activated by the majority of users. Therefore, the acceptance of such systems could possibly be improved by avoiding visual warnings (at least on the main display) and by employing tactile warnings instead. On the other hand, warnings which are especially noticeable, should be further investigated, it may be that although users do not prefer such warnings, but they react faster or more precisely to them. Tactile feedback lacks the possibility to be easily distinguishable between different event and thus even wished by the users is not suitable.

4.5   Reaction Time

In this section we evaluate the users' reaction time and the best warning modality and representation.

Warnings Obstacle Course

The response times were calculated from the time the warning appeared on the test persons display until the test person responded and looked up (see Table 4). The analysis of the collected data showed significant differences in response times between auditory and visual (p-value 0.000715) and auditory-visual/

Table 4. Average reaction times (standard deviations in brackets) for different warning modalities.

Auditory	Visual	Multimodal
0.74 (0.84)	1.57 (0.79)	0.44 (0.26)

multimodal and visual (p-value 5.96e-08) warnings. The auditory-visual (multimodal) warning caused the shortest reaction time but on a significance level of $\alpha = 0.05$ there was no significant difference between the auditory and multimodal warning.

Of the 29 test persons (only group *Modality* was tested) 2 did not see the hazard in the case where no warning was presented. In a real situation this could have caused a serious accident. In general, the evaluation of the videos revealed that the subjects were confused by the event and the non-existent warning and reacted relatively late.

Visual Warnings Terminal-Based

After investigating various modalities of warnings in the real-life scenario, a second, computer-based test, in form of a reaction test, was used to compare the values in order to determine the type of warnings which had the shortest reaction times, regardless of events and the obstacle course. Additionally various gradations of specific or unspecific visual warnings and spatial abstract auditory warnings or auditory icons were shown to the test persons. Participants had to decide whether the presented hazard was to the right or left of them and then react with their arrow keys. The time that the test persons needed from obtaining the warning until pressing the arrow key was determined as the reaction time.

In order to find an effective warning representation, we examined different visual warnings. On the one hand, these were non-specific (Group 1) or specific (Group 2) and on the other hand they were provided with different presentations for directions—arrow above (a), arrow below (b), arrow inside (c), text instead (d). Example visualizations are presented in Fig. 1. Since text can potentially reduce response times, it must be examined how subjects react to arrows compared to text. As possible additional text, the signal words according to ANSI Z535.4 [15] were used in conjunction with information of the direction and type of danger.

Table 5. Comparison in reaction time (in seconds) for different visual warnings.

Group	Mean	Median	Standard deviation
1A	1.215	0.866	1.059
1B	1.231	0.900	1.080
1C	1.545	0.950	1.055
1D	1.529	1.267	0.837
2A	1.142	0.883	0.952
2B	1.250	0.917	0.955
2C	1.390	0.975	0.909
2D	1.476	1.233	1.046

Table 6. Comparison in reaction time (in seconds) for auditory warnings.

Group	Mean	Median	Standard deviation
1	0.62	0.57	0.26
2	0.71	0.57	0.27

The results of the reaction time test, see Table 5, showed no significant difference between specific and non-specific icons, but there were differences in response times between either additional text or arrows that point out the movement of the hazard. Text had significantly slower reaction times in contrast to every other group. The position of the arrow did not change reaction times significantly. The test also showed that the concept of the direction-of-motion arrow according to DIN ISO 3864-3: 2012-11 [14] was not instinctively understood by about half of the subjects, and they perceived the arrows as position arrows. This misinterpretation of the sign direction is very critical because it could lead to real hazard.

Auditory Warnings Terminal-Based

To compare the visual warnings with different forms of auditive warnings we used abstract sounds (Group 1) and auditory icons (Group 2). You can see from Table 6 that auditory icons have significantly slower reaction times than abstract sounds (p-value: 0.001427).

You can see from the collected data, as for example the median (see Table 6), that the reaction times were slightly slower in group 2 than in group 1. Auditory icons had significantly slower reaction times than the abstract sounds (p-value: 0.001427). However, it is noticeable, that response times of two auditory icons within group 2 were significantly faster on the basis of a significance level of $\alpha = 0.05$ than the remaining auditory icons. Both sounds do not differ significantly in their response times from the abstract sounds (wilcoxon rank sum test). We neglect the differences between the different audio warnings, since the auditory icons have worked very well and badly partly. This is probably due to the nature of the icons themselves and thus not to the type of warning.

Comparison Obstacle Course with Terminal-Based Tests

The comparison in Table 7 shows that there are differences between the obstacle course and the terminal-based reaction times in case of visual warnings. In the case of auditory warnings there are no differences. In all test setups visually warnings were significantly slower than auditory warnings (obstacle course p-value 0.000715, terminal-based test p-value 2.2e-16).

Table 7. Comparison in reaction time (in seconds) for different warnings.

Modality	Mean	Median	Standard deviation
Obstacle course visual warning	1.58	1.47	0.79
Terminal-based visual warning	1.38	1.08	1.15
Obstacle course auditory warning	0.75	0.60	0.84
Terminal-based auditory warning	0.69	0.62	0.56

4.6 Legal Regulation

46% of the test particulates gave a positive answer to the question *It has been proven that distracted pedestrians by their smartphone can put themselves and others in dangerous situations. Would you sanction such behavior?* The interesting thing is that the *Warning* Group again, shows similar tendencies as shown in acceptance results, participants which received warnings would prohibit the use of smartphones in public spaces rather than the group without warnings. Thus, this approval seems to prove, that the sensitivity to the topic (dangers of distracted walking) has been increased by using a working system.

In addition, we also asked the participants how they would penalize the use of smartphones in public spaces. Fines were at the top with 72%, followed by freezing the smartphone as soon as the user moves (28%). These results are interesting since a big part of the participants (3.7) approve that smartphone usage while walking could be dangerous and all the participants use their smartphone at least sometimes while walking. Again, this behaviour can be explained by the difference between self-perception and perception of others. Participants probably do not assume they would not be affected by any sanctions.

5   Conclusion

We have investigated the willingness of smartphone users to use safety applications and to be warned by them in potentially dangerous situations. We found that approximately half of the participants would be willing to use such an application. While half the users might seem to be low, in comparison to other apps, this is indeed a rather high number and has the potential to become the next big established application.

By comparing the auditive and visual modalities shows that auditive cues are significantly faster. A multimodal (auditive and visual) warning is faster than either the auditive or the visual modality alone. The following reaction time test showed that there were no significant differences in response times between specific or unspecific icons. In both groups, warnings with text showed significantly slower reaction times than warnings with arrows instead of text. The position of the arrows had no effect on the reaction time of the subjects, but in the questionnaire, the participants mostly wanted movement direction arrows within, this means as part of the respective icon. For auditory warnings, spatial auditory icons have resulted in significantly slower response times than spatial abstract sounds. However, if one looked at individual tested auditory icons, they had no significantly poorer reaction times than the abstract warnings. It can be concluded from this that the nature of the auditory icons has an influence on the reaction times of the subjects.

We also want to point out that fully trusting and relying on safety systems might bring new dangers: people think they no longer have to be aware of their surroundings because they believe the system is 'watching for them'. However, the sensors or pattern recognition applications could malfunction or be turned off. This study focused on the user's perspective. Of course, the technical aspects play a very important role and, above all, in the field of safety, these must be reliable. Today's systems are not very sophisticated and maybe not convincing in terms of accuracy, but in the long run we believe that today's limitations can be overcome. Our study showed that users would adopt a warning system, so the challenge now is to find a feasible technical solution for providing it.

Wouldn't any prevented accident, harmful or not, be a very good reason to further develop and use such systems?

References

1. Priceonomics: The tragic data behind selfie fatalities. https://priceonomics.com/the-tragic-data-behind-selfie-fatalities/
2. The Guardian: Hawaii law targets smartphone zombies with crosswalk ban. https://www.theguardian.com/us-news/2017/jul/28/hawaii-law-targets-smartphone-zombies-with-crosswalk-ban/
3. Beuck, S., Scheurer, A., Wölfel, M.: Willingness of distracted smartphone users on the move to be interrupted in potentially dangerous situations. In: Proceedings of Cyberworld (2017)
4. Zhou, Z.: HeadsUp: keeping pedestrian phone addicts from dangers using mobile phone sensors. Int. J. Distrib. Sens. Netw. **2015**, 1–9 (2015)
5. Liu, X., Wen, J., Cao, J., Tang, S.: InfraSee: an unobtrusive alertness system for pedestrian mobile phone users. IEEE Trans. Mob. Comput. **16**, 394–407 (2016)
6. Wen, J., Cao, J., Liu, X.: We help you watch your steps: unobtrusive alertness system for pedestrian mobile phone users. In: 2015 IEEE International Conference on Pervasive Computing and Communications (PerCom), pp. 105–113 (2015)
7. Hincapié-Ramos, J.D., Irani, P.: CrashAlert: enhancing peripheral alertness for eyes-busy mobile interaction while walking. In: Mackay, W.E., Brewster, S., Bødker, S. (eds.) The SIGCHI Conference, p. 3385 (2013)
8. Pizzamiglioa, S., Naeema, U., Réhman, S., Sharif, M., Abdalla, H., Turner, D.: A mutlimodal approach to measure the distraction levels of pedestrians using mobile sensing. Procedia Comput. Sci. **113**, 89–96 (2017)
9. Nasar, J.L., Troyer, D.: Pedestrian injuries due to mobile phone use in public places. Accident Anal. Prev. **57**, 91–95 (2013)
10. U.S. Consumer Product Safety Commission: National electronic injury surveillance system (neiss) (2015). http://www.cpsc.gov/en/Research--Statistics/NEISS-Injury-Data/

11. Ipsos Public Affairs: Distracted walking study: topline summary findings. http:// www.anationinmotion.org/wp-content/uploads/2015/12/AAOS-Distracted- Walking-Topline-11-30-15.pdf

12. Haga, S., Sano, A., Sekine, Y., Sato, H., Yamaguchi, S., Masuda, K.: Effects of using a smart phone on pedestrians' attention and walking. Procedia Manuf. **3**, 2574–2580 (2015)

13. DIN ISO 3864–1:2012–06, Graphische Symbole - Sicherheitsfarben und Sicherheit- szeichen - Teil 1: Gestaltungsgrundlagen für Sicherheitszeichen und Sicherheits- markierungen (ISO 2864–1:2011), 6-23

14. DIN ISO 3864–3:2012–11, Graphische Symbole - Sicherheitsfarben und Sicherheit- szeichen - Teil 3: Gestaltungsgrundlagen für graphische Symbole zur Anwendung in Sicherheitszeichen (ISO 2864–1:2012), 6-32

15. ANSI Z535.4-2007: American National Standard For Product Safety Signs and Labels, 1–31 (2007)

16. Johnson, J.: Designing with the mind in mind: simple guide to understanding user interface design guidelines. In: 2nd edn. Elsevier/Morgan Kaufmann is an Imprint of Elsevier, Amsterdam, Boston, pp. 37–46 (2014)

17. Caplin, S., Campbell, A.: Icon Design, pp. 12–25. Watson-Guptill Publications, New York (2001)

18. Graham, R.: Use of auditory icons as emergency warnings: evaluation within a vehicle collision avoidance application. Ergonomics **42**, 1233–1248 (1999). https:// doi.org/10.1080/001401399185108

19. Familant, M.E., Detweiler, M.C.: Iconic reference: evolving perspectives and an organizing framework. Int. J. Man Mach. Stud. **39**, 705–728 (1993). https://doi. org/10.1006/imms.1993.1080

20. Gaver, W.W.: The SonicFinder: an interface that uses auditory icons. Hum. Com- put. Interact. **4**, 67–94 (1989). https://doi.org/10.1207/s15327051hci0401_3

21. Niewöhner, W., Ritter, S., Wickenkamp, D., Ancona, A., Briki, I., Koch, K., Markmann, M., Müller, D., Niewöhner, M: Fußgänger und ihr nutzungsverhalten mit dem handy/smartphone in europäischen hauptstädten: Verkehrsbeobachtung. http://www.dekra-roadsafety.com/de/fussgaenger-ablenkung-smartphones/

EEG-Based Mental Workload and Stress Monitoring of Crew Members in Maritime Virtual Simulator

Wei Lun Lim[1(✉)], Yisi Liu[1],
Salem Chandrasekaran Harihara Subramaniam[1],
Serene Hui Ping Liew[2], Gopala Krishnan[2], Olga Sourina[1],
Dimitrios Konovessis[3], Hock Eng Ang[4], and Lipo Wang[5]

[1] Fraunhofer Singapore, Nanyang Technological University,
Singapore, Singapore
{wllim2,liuys,scharihara,eosourina}@ntu.edu.sg
[2] Maritime Institute @ Singapore Polytechnic, Singapore, Singapore
{liew_hui_ping,gopala_krishnan}@sp.edu.sg
[3] Singapore Institute of Technology, Singapore, Singapore
dimitrios.konovessis@singaporetech.edu.sg
[4] School of Mechanical and Aerospace Engineering,
Nanyang Technological University, Singapore, Singapore
mheang@ntu.edu.sg
[5] School of Electrical and Electronic Engineering,
Nanyang Technological University, Singapore, Singapore
elpwang@ntu.edu.sg

Abstract. Many studies have shown that most maritime accidents are attributed to human error as the initiating cause, resulting in a need for study of human factors to improve safety in maritime transportation. Among the various techniques, Electroencephalography (EEG) has the key advantage of high time resolution, with the possibility to continuously monitor brain states including human mental workload, emotions, stress levels, etc. In this paper, we proposed a novel mental workload recognition algorithm using deep learning techniques that outperformed the state-of art algorithms and successfully applied it to monitor crew members' brain states in a maritime simulator. We designed and carried out an experiment to collect the EEG data, which was used to study stress and distribution of mental workload among crew members during collaborative tasks in the ship's bridge simulator. The experiment consisted of two parts. In part 1, 3 maritime trainees fulfilled the tasks with and without an experienced captain. The results of EEG analyses showed that 2 out of 3 trainees had less workload and stress when the experienced captain was present. In part 2, 4 maritime trainees collaborated with each other in the simulator. Our findings showed that the trainee who acted as the captain had the highest stress and workload levels while the other three trainees experienced low workload and stress due to the shared work and responsibility. These results suggest that EEG is a promising evaluation tool applicable in human factors study for the maritime domain.

© Springer-Verlag GmbH Germany, part of Springer Nature 2018
M. L. Gavrilova et al. (Eds.): Trans. on Comput. Sci. XXXII, LNCS 10830, pp. 15–28, 2018.
https://doi.org/10.1007/978-3-662-56672-5_2

Keywords: EEG · Human factors · Neuroergonomics · Maritime simulator
Mental workload algorithm · Stress · Brain computer interfaces

1 Introduction

Over the years, various methods and techniques have been established to address human factors research in improving maritime safety. Conventional methods such as statistical analysis of accident data and questionnaires can only be done post-hoc, and these methods risk overlooking outlier cases. Nowadays, instead of conducting human factors study onboard a live vessel, simulators are considered as different maritime scenarios can be reproduced. This makes it possible to assess the performance of different maritime cadets/trainees under similar scenarios. In our research, we employed Electroencephalogram (EEG) to evaluate human factors onboard a bridge simulator. This study extends our work in [1], where we studied workload and stress levels of crew members during task performance in a bridge simulator, using EEG-based workload and stress recognition algorithms. In this paper, we propose a novel mental workload recognition algorithm with deep learning techniques, which was tested on a database with 18 subjects collected in a maritime experiment described in [2]. The proposed algorithm showed improvement in classification accuracy compared to state-of-art algorithms and was subsequently applied to monitor crew members while they performed tasks in a bridge simulator. We also describe an experiment with 7 maritime trainees from the Maritime Institute @ Singapore Polytechnic with the purpose of studying the shared work among crew members. Workload, and stress levels of the trainees were recognized from the EEG signals. This allows the cause and effect of human errors to be studied.

The paper is structured as follows: Sect. 2 reviews methodologies in maritime human factors study. Section 3 introduces novel EEG-based brain state recognition algorithms, including novel mental workload algorithm and stress algorithm, which is based on the results from the mental workload and emotion recognition algorithms. Section 4 describes the proposed and implemented experiment, while Sect. 5 presents the experiment results. Finally, Sect. 6 concludes the paper.

2 Related Works

In this section, we first provide definitions of workload and stress which are the main factors to be recognized from EEG in this work. Then, we review traditional and EEG-based methods employed in the maritime domain to study human factors.

2.1 Workload and Stress

In our research, we refer to the term 'workload' as cognitive workload. Workload can be defined as the mental resource required to process information to complete a task [3]. Stress, as often discussed by academics and scholars, also has various definitions. It is thought that stress correlates with mental consciousness and emotion within a person when the achievable capacity is exceeded [4]. Both workload and stress are important factors in maritime domain for safety during cruising [5–7].

2.2 Traditional Methodologies in Maritime Human Factors Study

Many studies were conducted by analyzing available reports and databases which are usually a joint effort between the maritime organization and the government's safety department. The data from these case studies are often used to identify underlying common factors [8]. However, researchers face a major challenge as there is no standardized system to classify the type of accidents. Accidents usually happen due to multiple factors, and it could be difficult to categorize them to gain meaningful insight. One of the major problems to overcome is to be able to identify the common factors of human errors. These underlying human factors can originate from the interactions between environment, people or technology. Preliminary findings have also shown that human errors can be due to poor performance or lack of situational awareness. Given the complexity when considering the possible factors, it is difficult to identify the actual error [5, 8].

The administration of a questionnaire is a commonly used traditional assessment method. For example, operator workload is usually assessed with the administration of a questionnaire, such as the NASA Task load index (NASA-TLX) [9] or the Subjective Workload Assessment Technique (SWAT) [10]. However, this method only provides a subjective assessment of an operator's personal workload which might not be reliable. Furthermore, administration of such questionnaires is usually done after the task, which adds to the subjectivity of the assessment and is not practical from an operational standpoint, where the goal is to assess an operator's workload while the task is being performed.

2.3 EEG Based Methodologies in Human Factors Study

To overcome the problems encountered by traditional methods in human factors study, different types of bio-signals can be applied. Among which, an EEG-based approach has the best accuracy. The EEG device monitors electrical activity within the human brain in a noninvasive manner via electrodes placed on the scalp's surface, with high precision of time measurement. In the case of EEG-based assessment, various brain states can be identified with a classifier trained in advance. Thus, when the operator performs the task, his/her brain states will be recognized based on the trained model and not through any subjective assessment. Furthermore, the EEG device can be worn throughout the task and brain states can be assessed as the task is ongoing.

In this work, we monitor the workload and stress levels of maritime trainees using the EEG. Currently, EEG-based workload recognition algorithms which have the best accuracy are subject-dependent. Workload recognition generally involves the extraction of features, such as spectral power, from the EEG raw data and the subsequent application of these derived features to train a classifier. For example in [11], the researchers utilized a fusion of spectral power and event related potential (ERP) features to train a Support Vector Machine (SVM) classifier and achieved an average 85.0% accuracy for classifying 2 levels of workload. Other studies have also proposed using the combination of features from various physiological measurements aside from EEG. In [12], a study on a combination of skin conductance, heart rate, pupil size, EEG spectral power, and ERP features to classify mental workload was carried out. The average reported accuracy was 91.0% for differentiating high and low mental workload. More recently, deep learning methods are also being studied to classify mental workload. Research in [13] applied a stacked-denoising autoencoder to study within and cross session EEG workload data. Average accuracy of 95.4% and 87.4% was reported for classifying 2 levels of workload for within and cross sessions respectively.

In summary, EEG shows a great potential to be used in human factor studies for maritime applications. However, the development of EEG-based tools to study human factors is still in its infancy. Existing works can only identify limited types of brain states and there is little exploration regarding stress recognition. In this paper, we propose a novel mental workload recognition algorithm that can recognize up to 4 levels of workload and describe a stress recognition algorithm that can recognize 12 levels of stress [1]. We also proposed and carried out an experiment to study collaborative performance of maritime trainees in a bridge simulator. The details of the algorithms, experiment, and results are presented in the following sections.

3 EEG-Based Brain States Monitoring

EEG-based brain state recognition algorithms generally consist of two parts: feature extraction and classification. In the feature extraction step, different types of features are extracted from the raw EEG data. These features are then passed to a classifier to train a model, which can be done in a subject-dependent or a subject-independent manner. In our work, we propose a novel subject-dependent recognition algorithm, where individual classifiers must be trained for each subject, to obtain better accuracy. In the following sub-sections, algorithms for EEG-based workload recognition and stress recognition are described.

3.1 Workload

In this section, we present a novel subject-dependent mental workload recognition algorithm which uses deep learning techniques that outperforms the state-of-art algorithm. As mentioned above, the algorithm is subject-dependent and thus requires calibration for each subject. Given the requirement of recognizing 4 levels of workload in this maritime human factors study, EEG data recorded during a Stroop color word test with 4 different levels of difficulty was used to calibrate the classifier. The increasing level of workload is indicated by numbers as in Table 1: 0, 1, 2 and 3. These numbers correspond to no workload, minimal workload, moderate workload and high workload respectively.

For the Stroop test, level 0 corresponds to the subject observing the screen but not performing any actions. Level 1 requires the subject to press the correct key in response to the color displayed on the screen. The ink color matches the text displayed for this level. For example, the word "blue" will be displayed with a blue color. In level 2, the subject is still required to press the correct key in response to the ink color displayed,

Table 1. Workload states.

Workload level	State
0	No
1	Minimal
2	Moderate
3	High

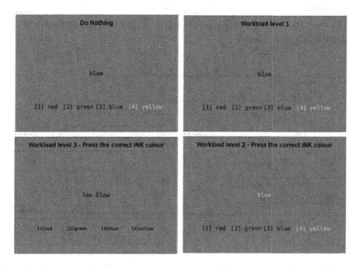

Fig. 1. Stroop test for 4 levels workload calibration. Clockwise from top left: Level 0, subjects are to observe the screen but not respond. Level 1, subjects are to respond by pressing the correct key corresponding to the ink color displayed. Level 2, same task as level 1 but with mismatch between word meaning and ink color. Level 3, same task as level 2 but with response time limit of 1 s imposed. (Color figure online)

but in this case, there could be a mismatch between the text and its color. For example, the word "blue" might be displayed with a yellow color, and the correct response would be to press the "yellow" answer key. Finally, for level 3, the task is the same as in level 2 but with a time limit imposed. The subject must respond within 1 s after the stimulus is displayed. The Stroop test interface is shown in Fig. 1. Each difficulty level lasts for 1 min.

To validate the performance of the proposed deep learning based algorithm, two different classification methods were tested using the same EEG Stroop test data from 18 subjects that was collected for workload calibration in a maritime experiment [2]. For classifier A, a SVM classifier was trained with a combination of fractal dimension (FD) and statistical features. The method follows the state-of-art algorithm proposed in a separate study on multitasking workload [14]. When applied on 4 levels of workload recognition from the 18 subjects, an average of 58.7% recognition accuracy was achieved from 5 folds cross validation on each subject. For two levels, an average of 83.2% recognition accuracy was achieved.

For classifier B, we proposed to use a deep learning technique, where spectral data derived from the Fast Fourier Transform of the EEG raw data was first input to an Autoencoder to learn a feature representation. The output of the Autoencoder was then combined with the statistical and FD features and trained with the SVM classifier. For this approach, an average accuracy of 79.9% was achieved from 5 folds cross vali-dation on each subject for 4 levels of workload recognition. For two levels, this approach gave an average accuracy of 95.4%. The classifier calibration process is further illustrated in Fig. 2. For both classifiers, all 14 channels were used and the features were extracted using a sliding window of 4 s with 75% overlap. The results show that the use of deep learning technique in the algorithm was successful in improving classification accuracy.

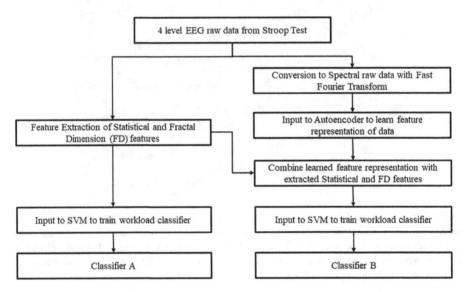

Fig. 2. Overall diagram for calibration procedures of 2 SVM classifiers used for 4 levels workload recognition from Stroop test.

3.2 Stress

There is still little research done on EEG-based stress recognition. Stress has always been associated with one's emotional state and workload level, as it is directly or indirectly influenced by both of them, with significant correlation being found previ-ously [15]. In this paper, we applied the algorithm proposed in [15] to recognize stress by combining the workload and emotion states recognized from EEG. For emotion states recognition, we follow a subject-dependent algorithm proposed in our previous work [16]. Sound clips from the IADS database [17] were applied to evoke different emotions during calibration and a combination of FD and statistical features were used as the input to train the SVM classifier. Once the classifier model is obtained, it is used to identify the emotional state of the subject. All 14 channels were used in the algorithm, and the features were extracted using a sliding window of 4 s with 75% overlap. We showed in [16] that up to 8 emotions can be recognized with an accuracy of 69.53%. In this maritime human factors study, we targeted to recognize 3 emotions: positive, neutral, and negative. The emotion labels and the corresponding numerical labels are presented in Table 2.

Table 2. Emotional states.

Emotion level	State
0	Positive
1	Neutral
2	Negative

Table 3. Stress states.

Emotion level	Workload level	Stress level	State
0	0	0	Low
1	0	0	Low
2	0	0.5	Medium low
0	1	1	Moderate low
1	1	1	Moderate low
2	1	1.5	Medium
0	2	2	Medium high
1	2	2	Medium high
2	2	2.5	Moderate high
0	3	3	High
1	3	3	High
2	3	3.5	Very high

We then apply the algorithm proposed in work [15], which combines the recognized emotional state and workload to get the stress level, as shown in Table 3.

4   Experiment

We proposed and carried out a pilot experiment to study the relationship between maritime trainees' mental workload and stress levels, and their task performance when they shared duties on the bridge of a virtual simulator. In total, 7 maritime trainees from the Maritime Institute @ Singapore Polytechnic were recruited. The experiment consists of two parts. In the first part, 3 trainees performed tasks with and without the presence of an experienced captain. The EEG data of these 3 trainees was recorded. In the second part, we recorded 4 maritime trainees' EEG data while they performed collaborative tasks. To our best knowledge, although this experiment has a limited number of subjects, it is a first attempt to investigate the brain states of trainees during collaborative tasks performance using EEG-based tools.

4.1 Simulator

The experiment was conducted at the Maritime Institute @ Singapore Polytechnic, which houses five full scale ship's bridge simulators. Each simulator contains high-tech equipment such as True Motion radar, Automatic Radar Plotting Aid (ARPA), navigation controls, and electronic navigational aids display. A 180-degree field of view is provided by large-screen monitors, simulating a highly realistic environment.

4.2 Subjects

In the simulator, each trainee was assigned to one of the following roles: an Officer On Watch (OOW), who is tasked with the duties of watch keeping and navigation on the ship's bridge (he is also the representative of the ship's master and has full responsibility for a safe and smooth navigation of the ship); a steersman, whose job is to steer the ship; a captain who oversees the safe navigation of the ship while giving instructions to the rest of the crew; and a Pilot, who is a mariner trained in maneuvering the vessel within congested areas or harbors, who also provides advice to the captain about navigation.

As the experiment consists of two parts, we had two groups of trainees. The first part was carried out with 3 maritime trainees with and without an experienced captain in the simulator. When the experienced captain was absent, the trainees took over the duty of Officer on Watch (OOW), Pilot and captain. When the experienced captain was present, the trainees took over the duty of Officer on Watch (OOW) and Pilot. The EEG from the trainees whose role is OOW/Pilot/captain was recorded. The duty of steersman was taken by other trainees whose EEG data were not recorded.

The second part was carried out with 4 maritime trainees in the same simulator. Each of them took up a different role to simulate actual bridge watch-keeping duties. The EEG from all 4 trainees was recorded. Their respective roles were as follows: Trainee 1 – Officer On Watch; Trainee 2 – Steersman; Trainee 3 – Captain; Trainee 4 – Pilot.

4.3 Experiment Procedure

Before the start of the experiment, the subject was required to complete an intake questionnaire. Next, calibration for the subject-dependent emotion and workload recognition algorithms was performed. As described in Sects. 3.1 and 3.2, sound clips from IADS and the Stroop color word test were used for emotion and workload calibration respectively. The Emotiv [18] device was used to record the raw EEG data when the maritime trainees were exposed to the stimuli, and the obtained EEG data was used to train the classifier as described in Sect. 3.

After the calibration procedure, the trainees were required to navigate the vessel in the simulator under pre-defined scenarios. Details of the vessel type and destination of voyage were given prior to the start of the exercise. Video was recorded in the simulator during the experiment in order to label the timelines of the EEG data with the corresponding significant events that occurred during the navigation.

5 Results of the Experiment

As the experiment consists of two parts, the results are presented in the corresponding two sections: (1) Trainees with and without experienced captain, and (2) Trainees collaboration with different roles.

5.1 Trainees with and Without Experienced Captain

The average levels of workload and stress recognized from the EEG of the 3 subjects are summarized in Table 4. It shows that 2 out of 3 subjects (Sub 1 and 2) experienced less workload and stress when the task is performed with the presence of an experienced captain.

Table 4. Stress states of the trainee with and without experienced captain present.

	Sub 1		Sub 2		Sub 3	
	Without captain	With captain	Without captain	With captain	Without captain	With captain
Average workload level	1.71	1.17	1.17	0.76	0.80	2.38
Average stress level	1.76	1.36	1.41	0.79	0.96	2.43

5.2 Trainees Collaboration with Different Roles

From the video footage, we observed the following three significant events during the exercise: (1) at 14 s, the pilot gave instructions to the captain and asked to reduce the engine speed. The ship was trying to navigate away from a stationary vessel. All trainees were alerted. (2) At 847 s, OOW identified a nearby ro-ro vessel, and cruise ship speed was identified as 6 knots. (3) At 1106 s, the trainees were discussing the voyage details. The brain states recognized from EEG signals for these three events are described and discussed in this section.

Brain States for Event 1. Let us first look at brain states regarding workload of the trainees during task performance. High attention was observed early on, from 2 s after the exercise started. Both the captain and pilot experienced the highest workload while the steersman had 0 workload level throughout this event. This observation was probably due to the captain and pilot having the highest responsibility in navigating the ship out of the congested area. As a whole, the average workload level of the captain was the highest at 1.63, which was of a moderate level according to Table 1. The rest of the crew members had minimal workload levels.

Looking at the brain states related to stress, the captain and pilot both displayed the highest stress levels while the steersman was at 0 stress level throughout this event. With reference to Table 3, the captain's average stress level of 1.63 suggests a low moderate stress level while the rest of the trainees showed a low stress level. The results for event 1 are summarized in Table 5.

Table 5. Brain states for Event 1.

		Workload		Stress	
Event 1	Activity during the event	At 14 s	Average (1–33 s)	At 14 s	Average (1–33 s)
OOW	Maintain watch-keeping duty and report to the pilot	0	0.27	0	0.28
Steersman	On the helms. Reduce speed of ship, navigate away from the stationary vessel	0	0	0	0
Captain	Receiving instructions from the pilot	1	1.63	1	1.63
Pilot	Giving orders and direction to the captain and OOW	0	0.50	0	0.55

Brain States for Event 2. In this event, the OOW reported the cruising speed of a nearby vessel to the pilot and captain after checking the navigation panel. We observe from Table 6 that the workload level of the steersman and OOW appeared to be at 0 most of the time, indicating that there is almost no workload for them. In contrast, the pilot and captain experienced moderate to high level of workload. At 847 s, the captain workload level was 3, indicating that he was having a high workload level when receiving instructions from the captain-instructor by phone. Meanwhile, we noticed that the workload level of the pilot was only at a high level from 837 s to 850 s when he was giving out orders. Thus, the average workload level of the pilot was 1.286 which was at the low to moderate workload level, while the captain had the highest average workload level at 2.571 among all trainees.

Table 6. Brain states for Event 2.

		Workload		Stress	
Event 2	Activity during the event	At 847 s	Average (837–857 s)	At 847 s	Average (837–857 s)
OOW	OOW identified the nearby ro-ro vessel and cruise ship speed as 6 knots	0	0.048	0	0.048
Steersman	On standby to navigate the ship	0	0	0	0
Captain	Receiving instructions from the pilot	3	2.571	3	2.571
Pilot	Giving orders and direction to the captain and OOW	0	1.286	0	1.333

Brain states related to stress levels for Event 2 presented in Table 6 shows that the steersman and OOW had almost no stress throughout this event. At 847 s, the captain's stress level was 3, showing a high stress level when instructions were received from the captain-instructor. Comparing stress levels across the event, a moderate stress level of 1.333 for the pilot can be observed from 837 s to 850 s when he was giving out orders, while the captain had the highest average stress level of 2.571.

Brain States for Event 3. During the discussion of voyage details at 1106 s, the OOW informed the captain and pilot about the route to be taken for overtaking the vessel ahead. From Table 7, the workload level was 3 for the OOW, likely as a result from processing the highly complex information to ensure safe voyage. The pilot gave advice to the captain after discussing the route to overtake the vessel, with minimal average workload level at 0.211. Of the entire crew, the captain had the highest workload level in this particular time frame with an average workload level of the 1.404 which is around minimal to moderate workload level.

Table 7. Brain states for Event 3.

Event 3	Activity during the event	Workload		Stress	
		At 1106 s	Average (1080–1136 s)	At 1106 s	Average (1080–1136 s)
OOW	OOW identified the nearby ro-ro vessel and cruise ship speed as 6 knots	3	0.351	3	0.368
Steersman	On standby to navigate the ship	0	0	0	0
Captain	Receiving instructions from the pilot	3	1.404	3	1.404
Pilot	Giving orders and direction to the captain and OOW	0	0.211	0	0.360

Looking at Table 7 for details on stress levels, we see that at 1106 s, both the OOW and captain had a high stress of level 3. Across the entire event, the pilot's average stress level remained minimal at 0.360 while performing the task of giving out advice to the captain on overtaking. Similarly, the OOW also displayed a minimal average stress level of 0.368. The captain, on the other hand, had the highest average stress level of 1.404, a medium value, during this particular time frame, likely from having to make key decisions about the route.

Overall Brain States. Across the entire exercise, to summarize the workload levels experienced by the trainees, average workload levels were calculated throughout the entire session. During all three events, the captain had the highest average workload of 1.71 as shown in Fig. 3a. Meanwhile, the rest of the crew had low workload levels: 0.45 for OOW, 0.01 for steersman, and 0.82 for pilot. The captain had the highest

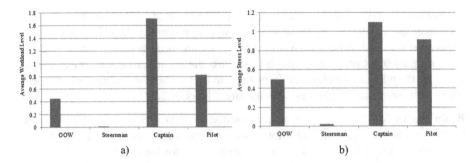

Fig. 3. Overall (a) workload levels and (b) stress levels for the entire exercise.

workload as he was required to give out orders to the crew and assume responsibility for the ship. As expected, the steersman, who followed orders given by either the captain or pilot, experienced the lowest workload level.

Stress levels across the entire exercise show the captain and pilot having the highest average stress levels, 1.097 and 0.918 respectively, as shown in Fig. 3b. In contrast, the rest of the crew had lower stress levels: 0.493 for OOW and 0.023 for steersman. A reason for this observation of higher stress levels stems from the need to give orders to the crew as a captain, and that both the captain and pilot are in a position of higher responsibility. Similar to the workload result, the steersman had the lowest stress level among all trainees at 0.023 as he just needed to follow orders.

6   Conclusion

In this paper, we designed and implemented an experiment to study workload and stress levels of crew members performing collaborative tasks in a maritime virtual simulator. To improve the accuracy of the experiment data analyses, we proposed a novel EEG-based mental workload recognition algorithm using deep learning techniques and applied it to identify the workload and stress of maritime trainees. The proposed algorithm was tested on a database with 18 subjects collected in a maritime experiment described in [2], which gave improved performance of 20% for 4 levels of workload recognition, compared to the state-of art algorithm described in [14]. The results of our collaborative experiment implemented in the maritime simulator showed the following: (1) 2 out of 3 trainees had less workload and stress when there was a captain to share their work, (2) the trainee who played the role of the captain experienced the highest workload and stress levels compared to the others, while the steersman had the lowest workload and stress. These findings are consistent in relation to the complexity levels of their roles. Both parts of the experiment support the use of EEG signals in monitoring the brain states of maritime trainees. In the next step of our study, we plan to recruit real crews from actual maritime companies and to shift the experiment design towards practical deployment.

Finally, the proposed mental workload and stress algorithms and the EEG-based human factors study method can also be applied far beyond the maritime domain. The EEG-based human factors evaluation tools described can alternatively be used for human-machine interaction assessment in the automotive industry, air-traffic control systems, user interfaces, game industry, neuromarketing, etc.

Acknowledgment. This research is supported by Singapore Maritime Institute and by the National Research Foundation, Prime Minister's Office, Singapore under its International Research Centres in Singapore Funding Initiative. We would like to acknowledge the final year project students of School of MAE of Nanyang Technological University and personally Lee Jian Wei for his contribution in this work.

References

1. Liu, Y., et al.: EEG-based mental workload and stress recognition of crew members in maritime virtual simulator: a case study. In: International Conference on Cyberworlds Chester (2017)
2. Liu, Y., et al.: Human factors evaluation in maritime virtual simulators using mobile EEG-based neuroimaging. In: Transdisciplinary Engineering: A Paradigm Shift: Proceedings of the 24th ISPE Inc. International Conference on Transdisciplinary Engineering, 10–14 July 2017. IOS Press (2017)
3. Berka, C., et al.: EEG correlates of task engagement and mental workload in vigilance, learning, and memory tasks. Aviat. Space Environ. Med. **78**(5), B231–B244 (2007)
4. Folkman, S.: Stress: appraisal and coping. In: Gellman, M.D., Turner, J.R. (eds.) Encyclopedia of Behavioral Medicine. Springer, New York (2013). https://doi.org/10.1007/978-1-4419-1005-9
5. Hetherington, C., Flin, R., Mearns, K.: Safety in shipping: the human element. J. Saf. Res. **37**(4), 401–411 (2006)
6. Arenius, M., Athanassiou, G., Sträter, O.: Systemic assessment of the effect of mental stress and strain on performance in a maritime ship-handling simulator. IFAC Proc. Vol. **43**(13), 43–46 (2010)
7. Lützhöft, M.H., Dekker, S.W.: On your watch: automation on the bridge. J. Navig. **55**(01), 83–96 (2002)
8. Baker, C.C., Seah, A.K.: Maritime accidents and human performance: the statistical trail. In: MarTech Conference, Singapore (2004)
9. Hart, S.G., Staveland, L.E.: Development of NASA-TLX (Task Load Index): results of empirical and theoretical research. In: Hancock, P.A., Meshkati, N. (eds.) Advances in Psychology, pp. 139–183. North-Holland, Amsterdam (1988)
10. Reid, G.B., Nygren, T.E.: The subjective workload assessment technique: a scaling procedure for measuring mental workload. Adv. Psychol. **52**, 185–218 (1988)
11. Brouwer, A.-M., et al.: Estimating workload using EEG spectral power and ERPs in the n-back task. J. Neural Eng. **9**(4), 045008 (2012)
12. Hogervorst, M.A., Brouwer, A.-M., van Erp, J.B.: Combining and comparing EEG, peripheral physiology and eye-related measures for the assessment of mental workload. Front. Neurosci. **8**, 322 (2014)
13. Yin, Z., Zhang, J.: Cross-session classification of mental workload levels using EEG and an adaptive deep learning model. Biomed. Signal Process. Control **33**, 30–47 (2017)

14. Lim, W.L., et al.: EEG-based mental workload recognition related to multitasking. In: Proceeding of the International Conference on Information, Communications and Signal Processing (ICICS) (2015)
15. Hou, X., et al.: CogniMeter: EEG-based emotion, mental workload and stress visual monitoring. In: International Conference on Cyberworlds (2015)
16. Liu, Y., Sourina, O.: Real-time subject-dependent EEG-based emotion recognition algorithm. In: Gavrilova, M.L., Tan, C.J.K., Mao, X., Hong, L. (eds.) Transactions on Computational Science XXIII. LNCS, vol. 8490, pp. 199–223. Springer, Heidelberg (2014). https://doi.org/10.1007/978-3-662-43790-2_11
17. Bradley, M.M., Lang, P.J.: The International Affective Digitized Sounds, 2nd edn., IADS-2. Affective Ratings of Sounds and Instruction Manual, University of Florida, Gainesville (2007)
18. Emotiv. http://www.emotiv.com

An Approach for Detecting Web
Defacement with Self-healing Capabilities

Mfundo Masango$^{(\boxtimes)}$, Francois Mouton, Palesa Antony, and Bokang Mangoale

Command, Control and Information Warfare, Defence, Peace, Safety and Security,
Council for Scientific and Industrial Research, Pretoria, South Africa
{mmasango1,pantony,bmangoale}@csir.co.za, moutonf@gmail.com

Abstract. Websites have become a form of information distribution; usage of websites has seen a significant rise in the amount of information circulated on the Internet. Some businesses have created websites that display services the business renders or information about that particular product; businesses make use of the Internet to expand business opportunities or advertise the services they render on a global scale. This does not only apply to businesses. Other entities such as celebrities, socialites, bloggers and vloggers are using the Internet to expand personal or business opportunities too. These entities make use of websites that are hosted by a web host. The contents of the website is stored on a web server. However, not all websites undergo penetration testing which leads to them being vulnerable. Penetration testing is a costly exercise that most companies or website owners find they cannot afford. With web defacement still one of the most common attacks on websites, these attacks aim at altering the content of the web pages or to make the website inactive. This paper proposes a Web Defacement and Intrusion Monitoring Tool that could be a possible solution to the rapid identification of altered or deleted web pages. The proposed tool has web defacement detection capabilities that may be used for intrusion detection as well. The proposed solution will also be used to regenerate the original content of a website, after the website has been defaced.

Keywords: Commands · Intrusion detection · Self-healing
Web defacement · Web monitoring

1 Introduction

The amount of information available on the Internet is vast. Web pages on the Internet support the dissemination of vast amounts of information, and render this information accessible on a global scale through a web browser. A web page is a document that is displayed in a web browser. This web page is usually part of a website, which is a collection of interconnected web pages. A website is hosted on a web server, which is a computer that hosts a website on the Internet [MEL1].

© Springer-Verlag GmbH Germany, part of Springer Nature 2018
M. L. Gavrilova et al. (Eds.): Trans. on Comput. Sci. XXXII, LNCS 10830, pp. 29–42, 2018.
https://doi.org/10.1007/978-3-662-56672-5_3

The information and content presented on the web pages attract a wide audience who are free to use the information for both benign and malicious purposes. Attackers target websites for a wide range of malicious purposes, including but not limited to defacement, personal financial gain, content manipulation and extraction of protected information [PE1, DE1].

Website defacement is still one of the most common attacks in cyber space [LE1]. The defacement of a website happens when the content of the website is altered or a web page has been visually altered. The altering of the content could result in the website being inactive. The common targets for this type of attack include religious and government sites, where hackers display a resentment of the political or religious views, therefore defacing the website to get their own opinion out there [CE1]. Figure 1 gives a visual representation on the reported number of websites that have been defaced from the year 2009 to the year 2017 [ZO1].

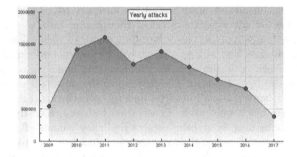

Fig. 1. Defaced websites from the year 2009–2017 [ZO1].

This paper proposes a Web Defacement and Intrusion Monitoring Tool (WDIMT). The WDIMT is able to detect defacement, authorize changes directly and conduct regeneration of a website's original content after internal penetration testing has been conducted. This will allow for the rapid identification of web pages that have been altered or deleted. Furthermore, the tool is able to rapidly remove any unidentified or intruder files. The WDIMT makes use of the Linux terminal for execution of commands that will access the tools capabilities. The web page has a graphical user interface, which gives visual representation of the files that are currently being monitored. The tool is not only used for monitoring the defacement of a website, the tool provides a possible solution to the amount of time it takes to recover the original contents of a web page. Furthermore, the tool has intrusion detection capabilities which allows the tool to identify any intruder files that have been inserted into a website.

The paper is structured as follows. Section 2 gives background on tools and techniques that were proposed prior to other research and the development of the WDIMT. Section 3 discusses the structure of the WDIMT which includes the system architecture, system requirements, system features, system flow diagram and the system usage. Section 4 discusses the analysis process of the WDIMT and proposes a scenario which illustrates the usage of the WDIMT. Section 5 discusses the advantages and limitations of the WDIMT. Section 6 concludes the paper and discusses potential future work.

2   Background

This section discusses related work which includes "Web injection attacks", "Implementing a web browser with web defacement detection technique", "Detection of web defacement by means of Genetic Programming", "A Web Vulnerability Scanner", "Countering Web Defacing Attacks with System Self Cleansing", and "Advanced Mechanism for Reducing False Alarm Rate in Web Page Defacement Detection".

Medvet *et al.* [ME1] proposes that "Most Web sites lack a systematic surveillance of their integrity and the detection of web defacement's is often dependent on occasional checks by administrators or feedback from users". Different website defacement tools have been proposed using techniques such as reaction time sensors and cardinality sensors [ME1,BE1].

2.1   Web Injection Attacks

Morgan [MO1] discusses code injection and specifically cross site scripting. Code injection refers to the malicious insertion of processing logic to change the behaviour of a website to the benefit of an attacker. Furthermore, Morgan identified cross site scripting as a code injection attack which is a very common attack that executes malicious scripts into a legitimate website or web application. Mitigating against code insertion is also discussed in this article, which proposes stages on how to possibly prevent code injection/insertion attacks.

2.2   Implementing a Web Browser with Web Defacement Detection Techniques

Kanti *et al.* [KE1] discusses a prototype web browser which can be used to check the defacement of a website, also proposing a recovery mechanism for the defaced pages using a checksum based approach. The proposed algorithm in the study was used for defacement detection; the algorithm was implemented in the prototype web browser that has inbuilt defacement detection techniques. The web browser would periodically calculate the checksum for the defacement detection technique's frequency which is based on the saved hash code or checksum for each web page. Upon comparing their algorithm against existing integrity based web defacement detection methods, they found their algorithm to be detecting approximately 45 times more anomalies than other web defacement detection methods.

2.3 Detection of Web Defacement by Means of Genetic Programming

Medvet *et al.* [ME1] discusses how Genetic Programming (GP) was used to establish an evolutionary paradigm for automatic generation of algorithms, for detecting web defacement. GP would build an algorithm based on a sequence of readings of the remote page to be monitored and on a sample set of attacks. A framework that was proposed prior to this paper was used to prove the concept of a GP oriented approach to defacement detection. A specialised tool for monitoring a collection of web pages that are typically remote, hosted by different organisations and whose content, appearance and degree of dynamism was not known prior to this research. Medvet *et al.* conducted tests by executing a learning phase for each web page for constructing a profile that will be used in the monitoring phase. During implementation when, the reading failed to match the profile created during the learning phase, the tool would raise alerts and send notifications to the administrator.

2.4 SQL-Injection Vulnerability Scanning Tool for Automatic Creation of SQL-Injection Attacks

Alostad *et al.* [AE1] discusses the development of a web scanning tool that has enhanced features that was able to conduct efficient penetration testing on Hypertext Preprocessors (PHP) based websites to detect SQL injection vulnerabilities. The MySQL1injector tool, as proposed by Alostad *et al.*, would automate and simplify the penetration testing process (as much as possible). The proposed tool utilises different attacking patterns, vectors and modes for shaping each attack. The tool is also able to conduct efficient penetration testing on PHP based websites in order to detect Structured Query Language (SQL) injection vulnerabilities and subsequently notify the web developers of each vulnerability that needs to be fixed. The tool houses a total number of 10 attacking patterns, if one pattern failed to expose a vulnerability the others would succeed in tricking the web server if it is vulnerable. The tool is operated remotely through a client side interface. MYSQL1Injector tool allows web developers, that are not trained in penetration testing, an opportunity to conduct penetration testing on their web database servers.

2.5 Countering Web Defacing Attacks with System Self Cleansing

Yih *et al.* [HE1] presented a defence mechanism that is based on high availability computing, which proposes that a backup of the server is available to immediately take over in the presence of server failure. The Self-Cleansing Intrusion Tolerance (SCIT) proposed, pushes the high availability computing one step further. A SCIT web server prototype was developed, that would copy all the contents and create a backup of the server. The SCIT periodically changes servers in order to generate digital signatures. These digital signatures are used to protect against defacing, altering of system files and web content. These signatures are recreated each time one web server goes off. This give attackers a difficulty of generating matching keys as the cleansing process is said to take 7 min. Using the signatures' integrities each time to conduct automatic detection of defacement triggering automatic switching of the servers. The SCIT web server is considered to be an additional layer of defence against attackers. In conclusion, the SCIT web server's design allows for off-line servers to be checked for integrity of web contents. The prototypes results showed that self-cleansing cycles are in the range of minutes, restricting attackers to a very short time window to breach the system and subvert web content.

2.6   Advanced Mechanism for Reducing False Alarm Rate in Web Page Defacement Detection

Woonyon *et al.* [KE1] proposed a mechanism for detecting any web page defacement that may occur on remote sites and introduces a method for threshold adjustment. For the detection mechanism, a feature vector for each page was generated by using 2-g frequency index. This calculates the similarity between the feature vector and decides whether the page has been defaced or not. The similarity calculation is done by comparing the current threshold with the threshold of the previous page. Dynamically changing web pages are also monitored for defacement directly from the remote site. The threshold hold method introduced, changes on a daily bases which is the then applied every second day. Within their experiments 185 web sites that were being operated in Korea were used. The rendered results show the variations generated by the threshold, identifying the similarity between the threshold and the web page. After the experiment, it was concluded that the threshold method was one possible solution to combating web defacement attacks, the detection of defacement was rapidly identified using the threshold methods that they discussed.

The proposed WDIMT makes use of the discussed concepts which include creating tools that may prevent and detect possible code injections, developing algorithms which are compromised with some form of checksum or hashing methods that will be used to detect web defacement, identification of any web pages that may have been removed by unauthorised personnel and regeneration of the original content belonging to a website that has been defaced. The proposed WDIMT comprises of functionalities used by the tools discussed prior such as rapid identification and notification of a defaced web page or website, regeneration of original content, rapid identification of intruder files and unauthorized changes made on webpages. However, the WDIMT is more client-side dependent, as a user has full control and view of each web page belonging to them. This tool also provides a visual representation of any new files that were added without the users consent, deleting them automatically which may minimise the injection of unknown/unauthorised scripts. Manipulated files or web pages are also visually represented allowing the user to easily identify affected files more efficiently. The response time of detection and reuploading of original content is rapid which may also serve as a preventative method for a denial-of-service

(DoS) attack on a website. Restoration of any deleted file or web page in the result of an attack, will be automatically regenerated.

3   Web Defacement and Intrusion Monitoring Tool

The Web Defacement and Intrusion Monitoring Tool (WDIMT) is a tool that will be used for website defacement detection. Making use of a website for displaying the current websites defacement status. Monitoring each website's web pages individually, automatic regeneration of defaced or deleted pages will be done automatically once the script is executed in the Linux terminal. The WDIMT can detect any defacement anomalies that have been made onto a web page or an entire site.

3.1   WDIMT System Architecture

The system architecture of the WDIMT is structured into 3 layers, seen in Fig. 2, presentation layer which represents the different graphical user interfaces that will be used for displaying the users information and the executions of commands in the Linux terminal; The execution of the WDIMT commands are not limited to being specifically executed on a Linux terminal; Business Layer where most of the communication between the database and the presentation layer occur, this layer controls the communication channels between the presentation layer and the data access layer; The data access layer displays the database which will store user information and the hash of each web page. The communication between the different layers is displayed in Fig. 2.

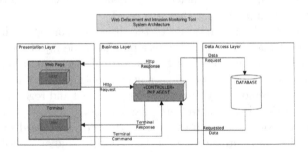

Fig. 2. System architecture of the WDIMT.

3.2   WDIMT Requirements

Using the WDIMT currently requires a user to have a Windows machine and the Linux machine. Both machines and the database were connected to the same network, this was done for immediate communication among the two machines and the database. The Linux machine is used to execute the commands and the

Windows machine was used to access the WDIMT web page for registering and viewing a user's data. A user has an option of using either a desktop computer or a laptop, or mixing the devices used.

The performance of the WDIMT may be hindered by the user not meeting the minimum requirements that have been defined. Processing time of the script may be hindered as the processing speed may be lower than specified in the bare minimum requirements. Response time of the database queries is another aspect that may be affected, as communication between the database and script could be occurring at a slower pace which is affected by the throughput of the system. These bare minimum requirements are to be used a guide lines for users whom would like to make use of the WDIMT. In the case of a user's system not meeting the bare system requirements, the WDIMT will still function but some the functions may take some time to process, store and request data from the database. For optimal performance of the WDIMT a user is expected to meet or exceed these minimum requirements.

The following section illustrates the minimum requirements for each machine: Linux Machine:

– Linux Ubuntu v14.04 or later.
– Hypertext Preprocessor (PHP).
– 80 GB Hard drive.
– 2 GB RAM.
– Intel Core i7 Extreme QUAD CORE 965 3.2 GHz.

Windows Machine:

– Windows 7 or later.
– 80 GB Hard drive.
– 2 GB RAM.
– Intel Core i7 Extreme QUAD CORE 965 3.2 GHz.

3.3   WDIMT Features

The WDIMT makes use of the Linux terminal for executing the script that will hash an entire site's web pages, the hashes are stored into a database. The database is hosted off-site, away from a website's web server. The hashes are used to calculate the hash of each web page individually every time the script is executed in the Linux terminal. The script will be appended with various commands that will initialise, verify, force and delete. In order to try and avoid any form of hash collisions, the WDIMT's PHP script has different functions within in to verify that there's no possible repetition of a hash. One function for getting file hashes is shown in Fig. 4. A user will be able to use the WDIMT's website to view the status of each web page which is represented by a colour schema on the website, green indicating that a web page has not been altered in any form, red indicating that a web page has been removed/deleted and yellow indicating that a web page has been altered as seen in Fig. 3.

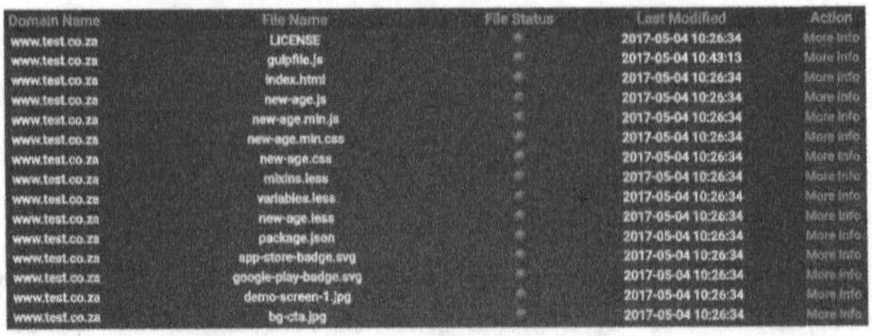

Domain Name	File Name	File Status	Last Modified	Action
www.test.co.za	LICENSE		2017-05-04 10:26:34	More info
www.test.co.za	gulpfile.js		2017-05-04 10:43:13	More info
www.test.co.za	index.html		2017-05-04 10:26:34	More info
www.test.co.za	new-age.js		2017-05-04 10:26:34	More info
www.test.co.za	new-age.min.js		2017-05-04 10:26:34	More info
www.test.co.za	new-age.min.css		2017-05-04 10:26:34	More info
www.test.co.za	new-age.css		2017-05-04 10:26:34	More info
www.test.co.za	mixins.less		2017-05-04 10:26:34	More info
www.test.co.za	variables.less		2017-05-04 10:26:34	More info
www.test.co.za	new-age.less		2017-05-04 10:26:34	More info
www.test.co.za	package.json		2017-05-04 10:26:34	More info
www.test.co.za	app-store-badge.svg		2017-05-04 10:26:34	More info
www.test.co.za	google-play-badge.svg		2017-05-04 10:26:34	More info
www.test.co.za	demo-screen-1.jpg		2017-05-04 10:26:34	More info
www.test.co.za	bg-cta.jpg		2017-05-04 10:26:34	More info

Fig. 3. The home page of WDIMT. (Color figure online)

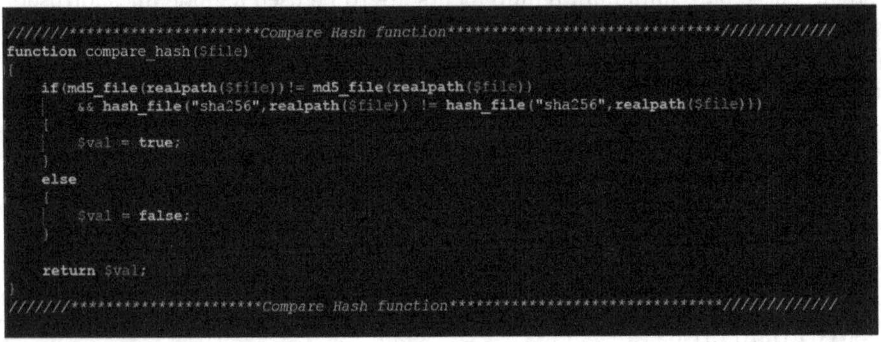

```
//////**********************Compare Hash function********************************////////////
function compare_hash($file)
{
    if(md5_file(realpath($file)) != md5_file(realpath($file))
        && hash_file("sha256",realpath($file)) != hash_file("sha256",realpath($file)))
    {
        $val = true;
    }
    else
    {
        $val = false;
    }

    return $val;
}
//////**********************Compare Hash function********************************////////////
```

Fig. 4. Code snip of a function in the WDIMT PHP script. (Color figure online)

3.3.1 Initialise

The initialise command is executed with a "-i". This command is used to read the full folder of a website, hashing each web page found, the stored hash will be used at a later stage by the verify command. A copy of the web page is also made and stored onto the database that is hosted off-site. The stored copies are retrieved when the original content of a web page is reloaded.

This command sets the status of a file to green and sets the reloading of the original content to a default value where the original content will not be reloaded. The reloading value may be altered by a user on the WDIMT web page.

3.3.2 Verify

The verify command is executed with a "-v". This command is used to verify the hashes of the web pages and check if any form of defacement has been detected. If the hash of any web page has been changed, the user will be able to identify the defaced web page of a particular page both on the Linux terminal and WDIMT web page as seen in Fig. 5. If a user would like to have the original content of the identified web page reloaded. The user will have to click on the "More Info" link. This link will redirect the user to a web page which has the functionality of changing a flag on the identified web page. The flag option gives a user the option of having the original content of the identified web page reloaded with its original content as seen in Fig. 6. After a user has selected that the original content of the web page be reloaded, the verify command will need to be executed once more in the Linux terminal in order for the status of the file to change from yellow to green indicating that the content of the web page has been reloaded. This command also has the functionality of identifying any intruder files and these intruder files are removed immediately. Any file that has been deleted is recreated and the file's status is identified by the colour red on the WDIMT's web page.

Fig. 5. WDIMT web page displaying a file that has been altered. (Color figure online)

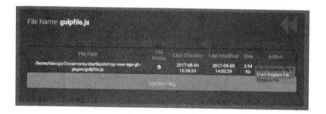

Fig. 6. WDIMT's web page with flag options. (Color figure online)

3.3.3 Force

The force command is executed with a "-f". This command overrides the verify command, as it reloads the original content of every web page. The comparing of hashes is used in order to identify any altered web page, the comparison process is executed within this command. Any intruder files that have been identified will be removed immediately. Files that have been deleted will be regenerated and all file statuses will be set to green. The command does not require a user to have the option of reloading the original content set as the command bypasses any option a user may have selected.

3.3.4 Delete

The delete command is executed with a "-d". This command is used to delete all the web pages that belong to a particular website that a user has specified.

This identifies the website's full folder path, a user has provided and deletes all the content that has been stored. This includes the copies and web page hashes that were generated when the initialise command was executed for the first time. This will clear all instances on the database. When a user accesses the WDIMT's web page they will have no files displayed to them as they have deleted all instances.

3.4 WDIMT Flow Diagram

The commands are in a sequential flow, with initialise being the first step required as the user will be registered and providing a path to the web pages that need to be monitored. Once the files have been successfully hashed, copied and stored. The user will be able to view the files that they have uploaded on the WDIMT web page. The verify command may be executed once a user has files uploaded. This command will check each individual web page for deface-ment, once defacement has been detected the web pages original content may be reuploaded. A user may prefer to delete their content from the WDIMT. The delete command will delete all the web pages that belong to a user. Furthermore the force command will execute the delete command followed by the initialize command. The flow diagram of the commands is seen in Fig. 7.

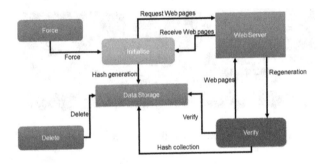

Fig. 7. Flow diagram of command execution WDIMT.

3.5 WDIMT Usage

A user will be required to use the Linux terminal where the user will be providing a full path to the location of a websites web pages which will be monitored. The Linux terminal will also be used for executing of the WDIMT script that will be run with additional commands for initialising, verifying, forcing and deleting of web pages belonging to the user.

After successful registration on the WDIMT website, a user will need to use a Linux terminal to execute the script with a initialise command, where a user will provide the full path to the location of the website's web pages as seen in Fig. 8.

Basic Syntax

```
php phpscript.php -e email -w website -s server -p path/to/webpages -option
```

Initialise

```
php phpscript.php -e email -w website -s server -p path/to/webpages -i
```

Verify

```
php phpscript.php -e email -w website -s server -p path/to/webpages -v
```

Force

```
php phpscript.php -e email -w website -s server -p path/to/webpages -f
```

Delete

```
php phpscript.php -e email -w website -s server -p path/to/webpages -d
```

Help

```
php phpscript.php -e email -w website -s server -p path/to/webpages - h
```

Fig. 8. Linux terminal commands.

4   WDIMT Analysis

This section analyses the data generated when the WDIMT's PHP script is executed in the Linux terminal. With the script being executed with different commands that have been discussed in the previous section. The following subsections makes use of a real-life scenario where a user will be making use of the WDIMT to monitor their website. Different outputs will be rendered during the scenario role-play.

4.1   WDIMT Scenario

This scenario shows that the WDIMT being proposed has capabilities beyond just monitoring of a user's web pages, regeneration of web pages after penetration testing has been conducted, and allowing users to visually identify the affected web pages giving full control over reuploading of the web page's original content. Different outputs will be rendered during the scenario role-play.

A user has successfully registered on the WDIMT's webpage. The user has also executed the initialise command on the Linux terminal and all their data is stored onto the WDIMT's database. The user executes the verify command to in order to verify if there has been no alteration to files or intruder files that have been identified as seen in Fig. 9. An unidentified intruder has noticed a possible vulnerability on the user's website and has been trying to gain access into the user's web server for malicious purposes. The unsuspecting user has been checking on their own website noticing that it is still fully functional. After successfully gaining access into the web server the unidentified intruder has successfully inserted some malicious files including a .exe file into the web server, that will be executed once the website is accessed by any individual. Upon accessing the website the files are executed and the following result is rendered as seen in Fig. 10.

Fig. 9. Intruder files that have been identified and removed.

Fig. 10. Hacked website results.

A possible solution for the user to render their website active again is to execute the WDIMT's verify command inside their Linux terminal. This command will generate a output for the user on the Linux terminal identifying all the affected files and even identifying and removing all the intruder files that were detected even the ones that have been inserted into sub folders. The user can access the WDIMT's website and change the flag option of all the affected web pages regenerated with the original content which was captured during the first execution of the initialisation command. This may be a time consuming operation for the user, a possible solution is to have the all the original content of all the affected web pages regenerated is to execute the force command which will override the verify command, which will remove all intruder files that have been identified. This will render all the statuses to green and regenerate all the original content of all files and web pages that were stored on the first execution of the initialise command.

5   Discussion

Numerous web defacement monitoring tools have been developed, offering different web defacement detection techniques. Some of these techniques are being

used in real life scenarios. The WDIMT has automated swift detection of defacement, swift notifications of defacement and swift reuploading of a web pages
original content.

The strength of the WDIMT lies in its swift detection of defacement of an
entire website's web pages, identifying each defaced web page individually, swiftly
notifying a user which web pages have been defaced. The WDIMT rapidly re-
uploads the original content of a defaced web page, visually identifies which web
pages were defaced and provides a user with flag options which will be used to
indicate whether the web pages original content should be reuploaded or left in
the current defaced state. The WDIMT availability is also a strength as a user is
able to identify the affected web pages on the Linux terminal without accessing
the WDIMT website.

The WDIMT has some known limitations. For example, the usage of the
Linux terminal for executing the commands associated with the WDIMT, this
will require a user to have a computer that has the Linux operating system
installed on it. This limits users that only have Windows operating system
installed on their computers. Authentication on the Linux terminal commands
does not require a user to authenticate themselves before executing a command,
this may raise security concerns as we are assuming that the person executing the
commands is the website's owner. Executing the commands requires a manual
approval rather than being automated.

6 Conclusion

Accessing the Internet has been made easier with the advancement of technology.
The volume of information that is being distributed on the Internet may increase
daily. With this information being accessed daily it is not likely that everyone
making use of the Internet may be using it for legal purposes.

The WDIMT is a web defacement detection tool that monitors web pages
for defacement, which makes use of the Linux terminal command which is used
for executing commands and a web page that will visually represent all web
pages belonging to a user. Upon executing commands in the Linux terminal,
the WDIMT will be able to detect any defacement that may have occurred
or is currently in progress. If any defacement was detected it will be visually
represented on the WDIMT's web page which gives a user the option to identify
a defaced web page and have the original content of that web page re-uploaded.
Swift reuploading of a web pages original content is one strong point of the
WDIMT.

The proposed tool encompasses most of the techniques and functionalities of
the tools identified in the background section. The WDIMT however adds its
own unique feature of swift reuploading of a web pages original content of which
most of the tools identified in the background that reach a level of identification
and notification of when web defacement has occurred. The WDIMT contributes
in bridging the gap of surpassing just rapid identification and notification of
any defacement that may occur, this tool identifies, notifies and regenerates the

original content of any web page that has been deleted or defaced. The WDIMT aligns well with the scenario identified in the previous section, as the tool's full capacity and all its features are used in fulfilment of the identified scenario.

Future work will be done on the WDIMT to allow the commands to be executable on a Windows machine. An impact study will be done using data gathered from the usage of the WDIMT. This gathered data may be used for analytic purposes that may assist in identification of which web pages get commonly defaced. For future avenues of research, it would be useful for a user to be able to have a mobile application that will allow the same functionalities as the WDIMT's web page.

References

[PE1]   Perez, T.: Why websites get hacked. Sucuri Inc. (2015). https://blog.sucuri.net/2015/02/why-websites-get-hacked.html
[LE1]   Lyon, J.: What are the 5 most common attacks on websites? Quora (2014). https://www.quora.com/What-are-the-5-most-common-attacks-on-websites
[CE1]   Cybercrime.org.za: Website defacement definition. ISC AFRICA (2016). https://cybercrime.org.za/website-defacement
[DE1]   Davanzo, G., Medvet, E., Bartoli, A.: Anomaly detection techniques for a web defacement monitoring service. Expert Syst. Appl. **38**(10), 12521–12530 (2011)
[KE1]   Kanti, T., Richariya, V., Richariya, V.: Implementing a Web browser with Web defacement detection techniques. World Comput. Sci. Inf. Tech. J. (WCSIT) **1**(7), 307–310 (2011)
[ME1]   Medvet, E., Fillon, C., Bartoli, A.: Detection of web defacements by means of genetic programming. In: Third International Symposium on Information Assurance and Security, IAS 2007, pp. 227–234. IEEE (2007)
[BE1]   Bartoli, A., Davanzo, G., Medvet, E.: The reaction time to Web site defacements. IEEE Internet Comput. **13**, 4 (2009)
[MEL1] Ninja86 L: What is the difference between webpage, website, web server, and search engine? Mozilla Developer Network (2017). https://developer.mozilla.org/en-US/docs/Learn/Common-questions/Pages-sites-servers-and-search-engines
[AE1]   Ali, A.B.M., Abdullah, M.S., Alostad, J., et al.: SQL-injection vulnerability scanning tool for automatic creation of SQL-injection attacks. Procedia Comput. Sci. **3**, 453–458 (2011)
[MO1]   Morgan, D.: Web injection attacks. Netw. Secur. **3**, 8–10 (2006)
[ZO1]   Zone-H: zone-h.org. Zone-H (2017). http://www.zone-h.org/stats/ymd
[KE1]   Woonyon, K., Jeongmoon, L., Eungki, P., Sangwook, K.: Advanced mechanism for reducing false alarm rate in web page defacement detection. In: The 7th International Workshop on Information Security Applications (2006)
[HE1]   Huang, Y., Sood, A., Bhaskar Ravi, K.: Countering web defacing attacks with system self-cleansing. In: Proceedings of 7th Word Multiconference on Systemics, Cybernetics and Informatics, pp. 12–16 (2003)

Assessing Opinions on Software as a Weapon in the Context of (Inter)national Security

Jantje A. M. Silomon[(⊠)] and Mark Patrick Roeling

CDT in Cyber Security, Oxford University, Oxford OX1 3PR, UK
{jantje.silomon,mark.roeling}@cybersecurity.ox.ac.uk

Abstract. Modern life is permeated by software which provides a large attack surface, ranging from generic, low impact malware attacks, to sophistically created and targeted code touted as a next generation of weapons. Although some research on this broad area of cyber weapons exists, the solicitation of public opinion through surveys is lacking. A questionnaire was conducted on the attitudes towards Software as a Weapon (SaaW), with this article presenting further results, linking traditional aspects of weapons to the understanding of, and differences between, software and malware in context of international security. The results suggest that there is a statistically significant difference between respondents in the *Military*, *Academia*, or *Other* professions concerning questions of capabilities, and the demise of the state-centric model. Furthermore, factor analyses identified eight dimensions in our questionnaire. Comparison of these across the three groups revealed significant differences in how peoples' background influenced their perception concerning the nature, intent, and potential of software and malware to be used as a weapon. Finally, using text-mining, we present the words frequently used to describe malware, software, and weapons, and provide an interpretation for overlap between constructs.

Keywords: Cyber weapons · Cyber security · SaaW · Malware

1 Introduction

Cyber weapons, digital weapons, virtual weapons, advanced persistent threats (APT)s, and software as a weapon (SaaW) are terms that are used frequently and interchangeably. Yet, they remain highly ambiguous, with requirements and definitions varying even further depending on the author. Although several papers, books, blogs and other media articles have been written on the broad area, ranging from technical analysis and case studies to potential consequences for the international system, surveyed public opinion remains absent.

However, such a survey is highly important: interconnected digital systems are vital to modern society, from personal use for communication and consumer transactions, to national energy supplies and security or international banking

© Springer-Verlag GmbH Germany, part of Springer Nature 2018
M. L. Gavrilova et al. (Eds.): Trans. on Comput. Sci. XXXII, LNCS 10830, pp. 43–56, 2018.
https://doi.org/10.1007/978-3-662-56672-5_4

and trade. Early in 2017, a global cyber attack 2017 intruded upon more than 200,000 victims in 150 countries within the first two days alone. It affected the National Health Service (NHS) in the UK, Deutsche Bahn networks in Germany, Telefonica in Spain, and the Ministry of Interior in Russia, to name a few. Experts warned of more imminent attacks and Europol's chief Rob Wainwright stated that the "world faced an escalating threat" [3]. The attackers' weapon of choice was ransom-ware called 'Wanna Cry', allegedly utilising the EternalBlue exploit developed by the National Security Agency (NSA) for a vulnerability in Microsoft Windows machines.

The advent of the Internet of Things (IoT) sketches out an even more data-driven and interconnected future, encompassing civilian aspects such as smart cities as well as military applications, with lines blurred far more extensively than before. Each individual can be a target, a steppingstone to the target or mere collateral. Equally, they can provide technical know-how or be merely an unwitting provider of resources and connections, thus acting as a key component. Lastly, an individual can also affect public policy via debates and elections.

This motivated the solicitation public opinion on these matters, with some results being previously presented [29, 30] of which this forms an extension. The work addresses the attitudes towards these weapons and how they are perceived to affect (inter)national security – all in light of three different groups of respondents (*Academia*, *Military* and *Other*). Furthermore a factor model with eight principal components has been created to, explaining 54.30% of the variance.

2   Related Work

Whilst the capabilities and implications of cyber attacks can be approached from multiple different perspectives and fields of study, the scope of this paper is limited. The following paragraphs will therefore only briefly introduce the most relevant related concepts and work.

2.1   Cyber Weapons, Virtual Weapons, SaaW and Malware

From a technical perspective, a myriad of work centred on specific aspects of malware defence and detection exists, addressing various elements such as botnet taxonomies [21], insider attack patterns [1], work on APTs [5,24,28] or classification based on code analysis [32]. However, the work rarely concerns itself with ramifications in the international arena.

Social and political sciences take a different approach: some try to firmly connect cyber elements to physical weapons that can be brandished [27]. Focus on a specific system, such as Industrial Control Systems (ICS) [26] is yet another debated topic, as are broader aspects, such as Critical National Infrastructure (CNI) and targeting [12,31]. At the same time, some attempt to create a wider framework [16,17] or address the topic of proliferation [14,15]. Yet others [19,23] debate the impact of matters pertaining to cyber security on statecraft and their subject-area, including a book discussing the theory, levels of cyber revolution and resulting strategic and policy based problems [20].

The legal community also discusses this topic, addressing for example the implications of using the term 'weapon' [6], overarching legal and strategic aspects of cyber weapons [25], examining the challenges they pose [7] or taking a step further and elucidating international law applicable to cyber warfare [18].

However, across the various disciplines, the main limitation of analysing these weapons is posed by their nature. For example, this might pertain to fundamental aspects, such as physicality and immutability. Or, it might address a more effect based aspect, such as destructive potential and tangible evidence thereof. Alternatively, it might consider proliferation requirements and (historic) data availability of a nascent area in constant flux. This is quite the opposite of the nuclear domain, which it is often compared to.

2.2 Deterrence, Nuclear Analogies and Public Opinion

Recent work drawing analogies between the nuclear and cyber domain often centres on concepts of war and deterrence. For example, [9] revisits nuclear war and the ideas of deterrence, escalation, and control but centres on the changes of the political landscape, also questioning operability in an environment of possible strategic or operational cyber war. On the other hand, [2,4] return to concepts of deterrence, the former discussing cyberspace deterrence strategy, whilst the latter analyses the lost logic of deterrence. The benefits and limitations of the analogy between the nuclear and cyber domain pertaining to deterrence have also been evaluated [10].

In regard to the importance of the individual opinion of SaaW, an analogy can be drawn to a discussion held in the nuclear domain several decades ago. In the early 1980s, the Harvard Nuclear Study Group published a book entitled 'Living with Nuclear Weapons'. The first chapter addresses issues in the nuclear debate, highlighting the importance of the individual as "each citizen is not just a target of nuclear weapons; each is also an actor in the nuclear drama" [13] before giving examples. This is also very true of the individual and SaaW. On the one hand, each individual can be affected: as a target, a stepping-stone to the target, or mere collateral. An individual can also provide technical know-how or be merely an unwitting provider of resources and connections. On the other hand, an individual can also affect public policy via debates and elections.

Yet, public solicitation on SaaW is often limited to media coverage, whereas the nuclear domain has seen the use of questionnaires and surveys since 1945, creating a wealth of (historic) data. The first series were carried out in the USA and addressed far-ranging issues, such as chances of nuclear war, questions about 'first use' or fall-out shelters. They also canvassed aspects of the arms race, weapon development, effects on security and the international balance. The wording, frequency and respondent base naturally varied over time, yet sufficient similarities can be found to ascertain common themes and perform analysis, an example of which can be seen in Kramer et al.'s work [22] from 1983, which evaluates nuclear surveys over 40 years.

2.3   Attitudes Towards SaaW

Previous work [29] presented results from the first two parts of the questionnaire, centring on concepts of weapons and the physicality of software. The core findings showed that although opinions on what constitutes a weapon varied greatly, there was some agreement: around two-thirds consider it to be an object that is offensively driven and is designed, or can be used, to cause harm or damage.

When deciding whether malware is a weapon, opinions were split; this was also the case when asked if a certain threshold is needed for this to occur. Members of the *Academia* group are more likely to disagree that software should be treated like any physical object, whereas as the *Military* group is more likely to agree and *Other* are indecisive, with the differences being statistically significant.

A clear majority believe malware can cause physical damage but there is disagreement as to what type of attack causes it to become a weapon (physical or digital damage), with differences between the *Military* and *Other* groups. It was also not conclusive whether the intent or effect would cause malware to become a weapon: on the one hand, most disagreed that damage mattered regardless of intent; yet, there was no consensus that intent is the decisive factor either. In both cases *Academia* members deviate more, particularly on the latter (intent) question, where it is statistically significant.

To get a better understanding of how these constructs (malware, weapon, software) are typically described and perceived, text-mining analyses is employed to discover informative words and compare these terms across constructs.

3   Experimental Design

The questionnaire design is the same as reported previously [29, 30] and it was conducted online. In total, 46 questions divided into three main sections were asked, following consent (Q1), demographics and topic familiarity (Q2–Q7). The first part (Q8–Q16) centred on more traditional aspects of weapons, their nature and constitution; the second part (Q17–Q34) moved onto the understanding of, and differences between, software and malware; these two parts have been presented previously [29]. The last section (Q35–Q46) shifted the perspective to the international security context [30].

3.1   Data Analysis

The respondents were predominantly British (61.5%), followed by Norwegians (7.3%), Dutch (6.3%) and German (5.2%) and the remainder split, with varying background as previously presented [29,30]. For analysis, three groups were used: *Military* $N_{mil} = 38$, *Academia* $N_{aca} = 19$ and *Other* $N_{oth} = 39$. Of the *Other* group, 10 identified as working in the IT sector and the remainder were spread, examples including those working in finance, hospitality or trade-crafts. The common five-point Likert rating scale including a 'neutral' response was used for the majority of questions. To ensure robustness, Mann-Whitney U (MWU) tests were used to test variation in value ranking between two independent samples. Non-parametric Kruskal-Wallis H (KWH) tests were performed to test median differences for more than two independent sample groups. Other questions were open-ended, although many were limited to "Any further comments?".

A Principal Component Analysis (PCA) was performed to better understand the structure in the questionnaire conducted. PCA identifies blocks of highly correlating items and combines these into components that explain portions of the sample variation. This was performed on all 41 quantitative items (questions) of the questionnaire (including subparts), fitting a model with factors which were allowed to correlate (Oblimin rotation). Sampling adequacy was assessed by evaluating the covariance among variables with the Kaiser-Meyer-Olkin (KMO) test.

3.2 Bias

In this type or research, bias may arise from various sources, such as response, interpretation or sampling. It is beyond the scope of this paper to delve into detail, particularly as dedicated discussions on the topic exist, for instance [8,11]. Here, examples of bias can include the (construct) validity of items and their response between different cultures and/or nations, the objectivity of norms, thresholds, and groups (three in this case *Military, Academia, Other*), the efficiency of the questionnaire measuring our constructs, and the unknown reliability of observed responses (e.g. over time or split half reliability). It is hoped that addressing the weaknesses and limitations of this questionnaire, as well as the resulting analysis, in the various sections is sufficient. However, an in depth psychometric evaluation could be an interesting contribution for future work.

4 Results and Discussion

A summarised view of responses per question can be found in tabular format in [29,30], for the first two and last part of the questionnaire, respectively.

4.1 Questionnaire Factor Model

The PCA revealed a 15 factor model with *eigenvalues* > 1, together explaining 74.17% of the variance. The KMO test was close to the 0.5 adequacy threshold (KMO = 0.497, $p < 0.001$). Initially, most factors included a very small number of items, with subparts of questions adding little information and thus being removed for subsequent iterations. One factor included Q10 – '*An everyday object or tool (e.g. a cup, a chair, a shirt) can be a weapon*' – and Q12 – '*There is no difference between an object being a weapon and an object being used as a weapon*'. To reduce the number of estimated components and because these questions do not directly assess attitudes towards software and/or weapons, they were also removed from subsequent analyses.

As items were removed due to their relatively small explained variance, the factor solution became more constrained and many items assessing overlapping constructs converged. Ultimately, an eight component model emerged based on the analyses of 33 items explaining 54.30% of the variation, as seen in Table 2. It assesses the following continuous dimensions (Table 1):

Table 1. Component interpretation and analysis

#	Component Interpretation	% var	Mean (SD)	F	p
1	Defining software/malware thresholds and capacity as a weapon	13.37	29.77 (6.43)	0.193	0.825
2	Perspectives on software/malware regulation, terminology, nature and effects	8.55	42.64 (5.71)	2.693	0.075
3	Weapon potential and role of software/malware	7.22	46.2 (4.64)	0.846	0.434
4	Nature, intent and potential of software/malware as a weapon	5.91	39.54 (4.94)	4.847	0.01
5	Topic familiarity and effects of software/malware capabilities on (inter)national security	5.44	23.14 (3.75)	6.654	0.003
6	Weapons use and software/malware capabilities pertaining to state security	4.88	43.25 (4.97)	1.521	0.229
7	Physicality of software and its effects on security	4.61	40.48 (5.12)	2.556	0.09
8	High level perspectives and attitudes	4.33	23.86 (3.18)	2.266	0.113

The table shows the proposed component interpretation, the variance explained by each according to the factor analyses, and the results between groups *(Academic, Military, Other)* testing with one-way ANOVA; Mean shows the group mean and standard deviation; F shows the ratio of between and within subject variation; p indicates whether F is significant.

Mean group differences (*Academia, Military, Other*) were tested in the eight factor model with ANalyses Of VAriance (ANOVA). Two of the eight scales (components four and five) contained significant mean differences between the three groups. *Post-hoc* comparisons revealed that in component four (concerning the nature, intent and potential of software/malware as a weapon) these effects derived from *Academia* (mean $= 42.71$, SD $= 4.77$) reporting higher values compared to *Military* (mean $= 38.55$, SD $= 4.16$) and *Other* (mean $= 38.91$, SD $= 5.2$) with $F_{(2,81)} = 4.847$ and $p = 0.010$. In component five, (assessing topic familiarity and effects of software/malware capabilities on (inter)national security), the significant group differences ($F_{(2,41)} = 6.654$, $p = 0.003$) existed because *Military* respondents provided higher values (mean $= 25.05$, SD $= 2.72$), compared to the *Other* group (mean $= 22.44$, SD $= 3.72$) and *Academia* (mean $= 20.33$, SD $= 3.81$).

Although the eight factor model explained over 50% of the variation and resulted in interesting/understandable/logical components, the KMO test indicated that the options with complex dimensionality reduction techniques are limited in this sample. The relatively low respondent/item ratio (96/33) could partially explain that estimate, as with a larger sample correlations are estimated with higher accuracy. Another step in instrument development could be to select the most informative items, thereby reducing the number items and the questionnaire length, potentially increasing its usefulness without losing information.

Table 2. Proposed eight-factor solution item loadings, after removing Q10, Q12, and suppressing factor loadings below 0.2 for clarity

Question		Component							
		1	2	3	4	5	6	7	8
27	Malware needs to cross a threshold to be considered a weapon.	-0.731		0.232					
29	Software/malware causing physical damage to a living being, a structure or system (a 'cyber-physical attack') is a weapon; software/malware causing damage to data integrity, accessibility and confidentiality is not a weapon.	-0.602		-0.335					
30	Software/malware causing damage to a living being, a structure or system (a 'cyber-physical attack') is a weapon, regardless of the type or severity of damage.	0.55			0.205				
31	The damage caused determines whether the software/malware is a weapon or not, regardless of the intentions of the attacker.	-0.546	0.205		-0.249			0.237	0.217
24	Malware is a weapon.	0.515	0.26				-0.273	0.233	
44	Software/malware capabilities can be clearly differentiated between civil and military applications	-0.394	0.235	-0.245			-0.346	0.312	
40	Software capabilities should be regulated globally, similar to the production and/or proliferation of other weapons.		0.679						
28	It makes sense to approach software/malware attacks with (traditional) weapon terminology (e.g. 'warhead', 'trigger', 'payload'):		0.636	0.202					
38	Software/malware capabilities provide a deterrent in general.		0.629				0.428		
36	Offensive software capabilities are vital to a state's security.		0.485			0.446	0.291		
39	It is possible to showcase software/malware capabilities without losing a technological advantage.	-0.403	0.424		0.305				
25	Malware can be used as a weapon.			0.722					
20	All malware is equally dangerous.	0.236		-0.684			0.2		
22	Software and/or malware can cause physical damage.			0.628					
26	Malware can sometimes be/be used as a weapon.	-0.442		0.585					-0.385
32	The intention of the attacker determines whether the software/ malware is a weapon or not, regardless of the damage caused.				0.83				
23	All software has the potential to become malware.		0.394		0.54	-0.29			
15	There are three types of objects: 1) those created for the sole purpose of being used as a weapon (offensively or defensively) 2) those created for dual use, either as a tool or a weapon, depending on the situation 3) those created to be used as a tool				0.376	-0.354	0.295	0.207	
7	Please rate your familiarity with the topic of international security:					0.748			
42	Software/malware capabilities have rendered state-centric security models obsolete.				0.375	-0.479		-0.443	
14	Weapons are only used offensively.						-0.722		
45	Software/malware exemplify asymmetric warfare.		-0.203				0.637		
35	Defensive software capabilities are vital to a state's security.		0.248	0.201		0.404	0.423	0.218	
43	Software/malware is a vital component of modern warfare.			0.292			0.348		0.231
18	Software should be treated like any physical object or tool.	0.342					-0.207	0.601	
33	Software/malware can be separated into three types: 1) created for the sole purpose of being used as a weapon (offensively or defensively) 2) created for dual use, either as a tool or a weapon, depending on the situation 3) created to be used as a tool				0.4			0.57	
6	Please rate your familiarity with the topic of computer security:			0.253	0.257			-0.539	
37	Software/malware capabilities lead to more insecurity than security in general.							0.482	0.43
34	Most attacks by software/malware fall only into three categories: 1) Mere nuisance 2) Summary offences / misdemeanour / petty crime 3) Indictable offence / felony							0.464	
16	If an object with an un-precedented destructive potential is created, but nobody is aware of it, it is still a weapon.		0.324						-0.546
41	Software/malware capabilities have propelled a vast array of new actors into the security field, nationally and internationally.				0.284	0.303	0.245		0.521
11	An everyday object or tool (e.g. a cup, a chair, a shirt) can be used as a weapon.	0.226			0.303		0.348		-0.499
46	An attack by software/malware can be considered an act of war.	0.229	0.294						0.295

Extraction Method: Principal Component Analysis; Rotation Method: Oblimin with Kaiser Normalization; a. Rotation converged in 90 iterations.

4.2   Software, Malware and Weapons

Three survey questions asked the respondents to define weapons (Q8), software (Q17) and malware (Q19) via free-text. In order to investigate commonalities of words text-mining was used, implementing *tdm* libraries and *wordcloud* in R. The answers were combined for each question into a string, which was then subjected to quality control, such as the removal of uninformative words 'the' or 'it', punctuation marks, standardisation to lower-case and the singular. Derivative words, e.g. 'destruction' and 'destructive', were re-coded into the word with the highest frequency. The frequency of all words was then calculated for each string to create the word-clouds seen in the figure below. The size of each word is determined by using the frequency as weight, after excluding any below three.

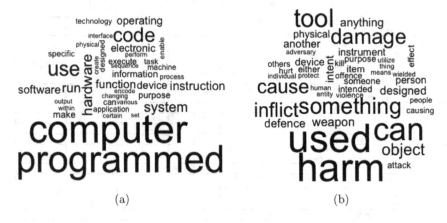

(a)   (b)

Fig. 1. Terms used to define: (a) software and (b) weapons

As seen in Figs. 1 and 2, there is substantial overlap between words used to describe software and malware as they both include 'computer' and 'programmes', with 'code' and 'hardware' that have a 'specific' 'function' or 'purpose'. The words suggest that software can have a broad function, including for example 'various' and 'changing'; malware on the other hand characterised by unique words, such as 'harm', 'attack', 'malicious', 'extract' or 'steal', 'information', 'negative', and 'damage'. The same overlap is observed between weapon and malware, with both being described by words such as 'damage', 'intent', 'harm', 'attack', and 'person'. Unique words used to define a weapon are 'hurt', 'physical', 'tool' and 'violence'. Overall, the text-mining analysis shows that a weapon and software are defined as predominantly separate constructs, whilst malware is defined as a construct bridging what we understand to be a weapon and software.

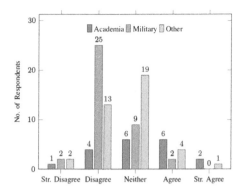

Fig. 2. Terms used to define malware (Q19)

Fig. 3. Software/malware capabilities have rendered state-centric security models obsolete

4.3 (In)security

No differences were observed between the three groups in the questions pertaining to whether or not software/malware capabilities lead to more insecurity than security in general (Q37), for a state (Q37a) or the international system (Q37b). Figure 4 therefore presents the combined responses of the groups to each of the questions. As can be seen, the majority of respondents were split between the neutral option and agreement. A reason for the former could be that the respondents believe the opportunities and threats essentially cancel each other out, or that there is sufficient robustness to accommodate for the changes brought by the new capabilities. The latter on the other hand might be acknowledging the new threat landscape, which disrupts the existing paradigm until some form of normalisation or adaptation occurs, thus leading to less overall security, as least temporarily.

4.4 Deterrence

Deterrence behaviour was long practised prior to it becoming a word in its own right, a field of study or a practice of international relations. It has come to be understood, in its most basic form, as preventing someone from doing something, though of course many nuanced forms exist. Within the context of states and international relations, deterrence operates on three different levels (a tactic, a strategy and as a vital element of the global (inter)state system) but a lay person is most likely to be familiar with ideas of military power or nuclear weapons.

When asked whether or not software/malware capabilities provide a deterrent in general (Q38), when displayed/visible (Q38a) or when implied (Q38b), no difference was found between the three groups. The results with combined groups can be seen in Fig. 5. A total of 14 expanded on their answers, which covered a wide spectrum and can be found in [30].

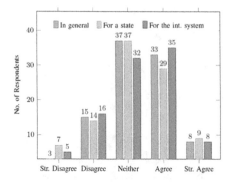

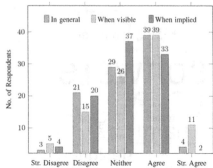

Fig. 4. Software/malware capabilities lead to more insecurity

Fig. 5. Software/malware capabilities provide a deterrent

Whether it is possible to showcase software/malware capabilities without losing a technological advantage split opinion, but not significantly between the three groups, with the largest proportion being in agreement, followed by those remaining neutral seen in Fig. 7(a). The option to comment further was taken by 18 respondents, five of whom stated that they do not feel sufficiently qualified to answer; three suggested that showcasing would be an incentive to replicate the said capability or that it should be possible to show an effect without detail/the code itself; the remainder are single responses, for example stating that it is assumed one has an advantage, that malware requires vulnerabilities/mistakes from others, or that some of the best code development comes from open-source systems.

4.5   State-Centric Model

There was a high level of agreement that a vast number of actors have been propelled into the security field, both nationally and internationally (Q41), as can be seen in 6(c), with no difference between the three groups. Yet, the extent to which these new actors have affected the traditional, state-centric model, is highly disputed. The largest divergence in responses overall pertained to the statement that software/malware capabilities have rendered state-centric security models obsolete (Q42) depicted in Fig. 3, with the KWH test showing significance ($H(2) = 13.979$, $p = 0.0009$).

More specifically, whilst the vast majority of the *Military* disagree, there is far less consensus within the remaining two groups: *Other* appears to favour the neutral response, but still has many disagreeing; *Academia* on the other hand has more in agreement than not, although also a large proportion of neutral responses. Statistically, significance was found *post hoc* using MWU, with *Military-Academic* ($U = 200.5$, $p = 0.0003$), *Military-Other* ($U = 482.5$, $p = 0.0052$), and *Academic-Other* ($U = 280.5$, $p = 0.0326$).

Additional comments (Q42a) were included by 16 respondents, six of whom can be summarised as believing that it has affected the model but not sufficiently yet to render it obsolete; five see states as still being the dominant element, and another four did not feel qualified enough to answer well. The last respondent asserted the model is constantly changing.

4.6   Software Capabilities and State Security

There is clear agreement across the groups that defensive software capabilities are vital to a state's security (Q35) as shown in Fig. 6(a). However, this is not the case when asking about the offensive element (Q36): the *Military* group most strongly agrees that it is vital, *Academia* less so, and the *Other* group the least, as seen in 5b. A KWH test underlined this finding showing a difference ($H(2) = 11.167$, $p = 0.0038$) between the groups; using MWU for *post hoc* analysis, *Military-Other*

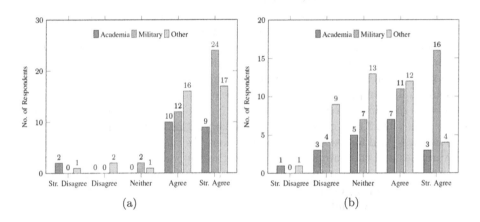

Fig. 6. Vital to a state's security: (a) defensive and (b) offensive capabilities

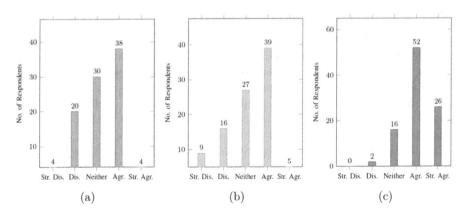

Fig. 7. Software/malware capabilities: (a) can be showcased without loosing technical advantage (b) need to be regulated globally (c) have propelled a vast array of new actors into the field

(U = 409.5, $p = 0.0007$) and *Military-Academia* (U = 273, $p = 0.0192$) variation remain significant, however *Academia-Other* (U = 339, $p = 0.2048$) do not.

Regulation of capabilities, akin to the production and/or proliferation of other weapons (Q40) split opinions, but without difference based on the three groups. Figure 7(b) shows how, whilst a large number are in favour, there is almost as much disagreement as those remaining neutral. Moreover, when asked to comment further, 35 chose to do so; the problem of enforceability was mentioned by 24, with other varied responses [30].

5   Conclusion and Future Work

This article presented the results of an online questionnaire carried out to source public attitudes towards SaaW, supplementing the academic discourse. Although a total of 46 questions were asked, this article centres on the questions pertaining to (inter)national security, text-mined comparisons between software, malware and weapons, as well as a structural analysis of the questionnaire itself via PCA. Results centring on the first two parts, including the nature and constitution of weapons and software have been presented previously [29].

Only fully completed questionnaires were used for analysis, giving a total of N = 96, split into three groups *Military* $N_{mil} = 38$, *Academia* $N_{aca} = 19$ and *Other* $N_{oth} = 39$. The common five-point Likert rating scale including a 'neutral' response was used for the majority of questions. As the responses were not interval variables and the sample sizes differed, the nonparametric Kruskal-Wallis H tests were performed to test median differences for more than two independent sample groups; Mann-Whitney U tests were used to test variation in value ranking between two independent samples. The PCA resulted in an eight factor model was created explaining over 50% of the variation, with interesting and understandable results. However, the low KMO test indicated that the options with complex dimensionality reduction techniques are limited in this sample, possibly due to the relatively low respondent/item ratio (96/33).

There is substantial overlap between words used to describe 'software' and 'malware' by the respondents. Whilst 'software' appears to be thought of having a broad function, 'malware' is characterised by unique expressions. The same overlap is observed between 'weapon' and 'malware', with some unique words used to define a 'weapon'. Overall, it appears that a 'weapon' and 'software' are thought of as predominantly separate constructs, whilst malware is defined as a bridging construct, connecting what is believed to be a 'weapon' and 'software'.

Regarding software/malware regulation, there is a tendency to agree across the groups, but also strong concern regarding enforceability. Whilst there is clear agreement across the groups that defensive software capabilities are vital to a state's security, this is not the case when asking about the offensive element.

The opinions on whether software/malware capabilities have rendered state-centric security models obsolete split the groups, with the differences being statistically significant: whilst a clear majority of the *Military* group disagree, the *Other* group tends to remain neutral or disagrees, and *Academia* is most disparate. Furthermore, there is agreement across the groups that these new capabilities have propelled a vast array of new actors into the field.

In a young and rapidly evolving field as cyber security, fundamental studies aimed at describing constructs and understanding the perception of important concepts in different populations are paramount. This study presents significant differences in the interpretation and perception of three basic constructs depending on the background and training of respondents, underlining the population heterogeneity in the understanding of the potential of software and malware of cyber weapons. Understanding this heterogeneity is important to prevent misunderstandings, reach agreement on definitions and comprehend the potency of adversaries in cyberspace. We hope that the standardised and objective nature of the assessment procedure proposed in this study contributes to more efficient and valid study of basic cyber security concepts.

Future work based on the data from this questionnaire, particularly the PCA, could be used to narrow down the questionnaire to 15–20 questions, for example by selecting the most informative ones based on the highest factor loading for their component. This would allow for a more efficient instrument that is not only more analytically viable but is also likely to yield higher response rates. The sources and effects of bias may also lead to an interesting contribution, for example in the form of an in depth psychometric evaluation. Furthermore, it will be interesting to conduct this questionnaire, or a streamlined version, over time to gain longitudinal data, and to observe the changing nature and attitudes.

References

1. Agrafiotis, I., Nurse, J.R.C., Buckley, O., Legg, P.A., Creese, S., Goldsmith, M.: Identifying attack patterns for insider threat detection. Comput. Fraud Secur. **2015**(7), 9–17 (2015)
2. Alperovitch, D.: Towards establishment of cyberspace deterrence strategy. In: 2011 3rd International Conference on Cyber Conflict, pp. 1–8 (2011)
3. BBC Technology: Ransomware cyber-attack threat escalating - Europol - BBC News (2017). http://www.bbc.co.uk/news/technology-39913630
4. Betts, R.K.: The lost logic of deterrence. Foreign Aff. **1**(87), 87–99 (2013)
5. Bhatt, P., Yano, E.T., Gustavsson, P.: Towards a framework to detect multi-stage advanced persistent threats attacks. In: Proceedings of IEEE 8th International Symposium on Service Oriented System Engineering, SOSE 2014, pp. 390–395 (2014)
6. Blake, D., Imburgia, J.S.: Bloodless weapons? Air Force Law Rev. **66**, 157–204 (2010)
7. Brown, G., Metcalf, A.: Easier said than done: legal reviews of cyber weapons. J. Natl. Secur. Law Policy **7**, 115–138 (2014)
8. Choi, B.C.K., Pak, A.W.P.: A catalog of biases in questionnaires. Prev. Chronic Dis. **2**(1), 1–13 (2005)
9. Cimbala, S.J.: On nuclear war: deterrence, escalation, and control. Mil. Strateg. Aff. **4**(3), 25–43 (2012)
10. Cirenza, P.: An evaluation of the analogy between nuclear and cyber deterrence. Ph.D. thesis, Stanford University (2015)

11. Fowler Jr., F.J.: Survey Research Methods. Sage Publications Limited, London (2013)
12. Hakkarainen, P.: Cyber Weapon Target Analysis. BoD (2014)
13. Harvard Nuclear Study Group: Living With Nuclear Weapons. Bantam Books, New York (1983)
14. Herr, T.: Malware counter-proliferation and the Wassenaar arrangement (2016)
15. Herr, T., Armbrust, E.: Milware: the implications of state authored malicious software. Soc. Sci. Res. Netw. (2015)
16. Herr, T., Dc, W.: PrEP: a framework for malware & cyber weapons. J. Inf. Warf. **13**(1) (2014)
17. Herr, T., Rosenzweig, P.: Cyber weapons and export control: incorporating dual use with the PrEP model. J. Natl. Secur. Law Policy **8**(2), 1–16 (2015)
18. International Group of Experts, Schmitt, M.N.: Tallinn Manual on the International Law Applicable to Cyber Warfare. Cambridge University Press, Cambridge (2013)
19. Kello, L.: The meaning of the cyber revolution. Int. Secur. **38**(2), 7–40 (2013)
20. Kello, L.: The Virtual Weapon and International Order. Yale University Press, New Haven (2017)
21. Khattak, S., Ramay, N.R., Khan, K.R., Syed, A.A., Khayam, S.A.: A taxonomy of botnet behavior, detection, and defense. IEEE Commun. Surv. Tutor. **16**(2), 898–924 (2014)
22. Kramer, B.M., Kalick, S.M., Milburn, M.A.: Attitudes toward nuclear weapons and nuclear war: 1945–1982. J. Soc. Issues **39**(I), 7–24 (1983)
23. Lindsay, J.R., Kello, L.: Correspondence: a cyber disagreement. Int. Secur. **39**(2), 181–192 (2014)
24. Liu, S.-T., Chen, Y.-M., Lin, S.-J.: A novel search engine to uncover potential victims for APT investigations. In: Hsu, C.-H., Li, X., Shi, X., Zheng, R. (eds.) NPC 2013. LNCS, vol. 8147, pp. 405–416. Springer, Heidelberg (2013). https://doi.org/10.1007/978-3-642-40820-5_34
25. Mele, S.: Cyber-weapons: legal and strategic aspects (Version 2.0). Italian Institute of Strategic Studies "Niccolò Machiavelli", 22 June 2013
26. Peterson, D.: Offensive cyber weapons: construction, development, and employment. J. Strateg. Stud. **36**(1), 120–124 (2013)
27. Rid, T., McBurney, P.: Cyber-weapons. RUSI J. **157**(1), 6–13 (2012)
28. Roth, F.: APT groups and operations (2016). goo.gl/MYkxhT
29. Silomon, J.A.M., Roscoe, A.W.: Attitudes towards software as a weapon. In: IADIS International Conference ICT, Society and Human Beings, Lisbon, pp. 119–126 (2017)
30. Silomon, J.A.M., Roscoe, A.W.: Software and malware capabilities: opinions on (inter)national security. In: International Conference on Cyberworlds, pp. 96–102 (2017)
31. Tabansky, L.: Critical infrastructure protection against cyber threats, vol. 3 (2011)
32. Wilson, C.: Cyber weapons: 4 defining characteristics (2015)

OpenGL|D - An Alternative Approach to Multi-user Architecture

Karsten Pedersen[(✉)], Christos Gatzidis, and Wen Tang

Department of Creative Technology, Faculty of Science and Technology,
Bournemouth University, Bournemouth, UK
pedersenk@bournemouth.ac.uk

Abstract. Synchronising state between multiple connected clients can be a challenging task. However, the need to carry this out is becoming much greater as a larger number of software packages are becoming collaborative across a network. Online multiplayer games in particular are already extremely popular but the synchronisation methods and architecture have largely remained the same. OpenGL|Distributed, presented here, aims to provide not only an alternative to this architecture allowing for a greatly simplified development pipeline, but also the opportunity for a number of additional features and design patterns. The architecture provided by OpenGL|D is such that no state information needs to be transferred between clients. Instead, the OpenGL API has been utilised as a platform agnostic protocol. This means that graphical calls can be streamed to each client rather than relying on manual synchronisation of application domain specific data. Initial test results are discussed, including performance evaluation using data from a number of small prototypes developed within a constrained 48-h timeframe. These results are compared and evaluated against a more traditional approach to network multiplayer by id Software's QuakeWorld client. It should be noted that this article is an extended version of the work we published in the proceedings of the Cyberworlds 2017 conference [1].

1 Introduction

One could argue that online multiplayer games are amongst the most popular entertainment media of the last few years. However, the software infrastructure to support these multiplayer games is very large and complex [2]. Issues regarding real-time performance of user interactions and graphics rendering remain challenging, even with today's state of the art software technology [3,4]. Common to multiplayer games are problems associated with server workload latency, scalable communication costs plus real-time localisation and replication of player interaction. Specifically, large-scale games involving tens and thousands of players require a range of solutions to address the problem from design and implementation to evaluation.

The most popular contemporary game engines such as Unreal Engine 4 [5] and Unity [6] are employing the centralized client/server architecture. Whilst

© Springer-Verlag GmbH Germany, part of Springer Nature 2018
M. L. Gavrilova et al. (Eds.): Trans. on Comput. Sci. XXXII, LNCS 10830, pp. 57–74, 2018.
https://doi.org/10.1007/978-3-662-56672-5_5

providing efficient state updates via players sending control messages to a central server, multiplayer games developed using this approach present some inherited problems in terms of robustness and scalability. With the increasing complexity of contemporary multiplayer games, the client-server architecture can potentially become a computation and communication bottleneck.

Further to the scalability issue, the centralized design enforces the game developers to rely on infrastructures provided by game engine manufacturers, which can prevent software preservation and reusability, an important topic that has been overlooked until now [7].

The rapid development and evolution of computer architecture often fails to provide an infrastructure in order to ensure that older software can continue to run on recent platforms. For example, the recent developments in Windows 10 S [8], to allow only Microsoft Store apps from being run, effectively fail to cater for many previous standard, well-implemented Win32 programs, which are still valid for many industry standard applications. Thus, the lack of infrastructure in place to cater for these sometimes mission critical software packages may cause a failure in the uptake of a new platform. Being able to run existing or legacy applications has the benefits of saving costs and reducing the risk of introducing bugs during the development of the replacement software [9].

In this paper, we introduce a novel distributed architecture for multiplayer games; OpenGL|D (OpenGL Distributed), which is an evolving attempt at addressing the aforementioned challenging issues. In addition to this, OpenGL|D is also aimed at improving the lifespan of software. In particular, through OpenGL|D, 3D software applications such as Virtual Reality (VR) and Augmented Reality (AR) applications are allowed to be run from inside a virtual machine (VM), whilst still benefiting from hardware accelerated performance from the graphical processing unit (GPU). This is achieved by forwarding the graphical calls from the virtual environment into a WebGL enabled web browser via websockets.

VMs today can be seen as one of the few solutions to running old software without needing to port it to a modern platform, and together with OpenGL|D, older 3D software can be guaranteed to run because of their use.

OpenGL|D can offer more beyond potential success in the area of digital preservation, as it can also open up new possibilities for the architecture of multi-user, collaborative tools and gaming software. Of particular interest is the fact that even though the graphics are processed on the GPU of the individual connected client machines, the software itself and the logic contained within is running on a single machine, the server. This means that each client implicitly shares a single application state which completely eliminates the need to synchronise the clients. This not only simplifies the development of multi-user network software but can also potentially reduce bandwidth [10,11].

Our contributions in this paper can be summarised to the following:

- A new architecture design and implementation of medium-scale multiplayer games, VR and AR applications
- A framework to allow games to be developed in a simple intuitive manner without needing to consider the complexity of multiplayer system design
- A platform agnostic approach allowing multiplayer software to be written and executed on any computer platform
- An innovative re-implementation of one of the industry standard graphics APIs, OpenGL, allowing a drop-in replacement to help integration with existing projects

In the following sections we first describe the existing solutions to the synchronisation of multiplayer games. We then provide further details and examples of the complexities involved in client side synchronisation, which illustrate a number of scenarios that developers will be faced with during the development process of multi-user/multiplayer software, and, subsequently, how a new approach will improve upon the ways of traditional architectures. We then describe the design of OpenGL|D in Sect. 4. Performance evaluation is presented in Sect. 5. Finally, we point out some future developments for the extended use of OpenGL|D in both research and development projects.

2 Related Work in Client Synchronisation

Existing online multiplayer games utilize a client-server model which not only introduces latency but also a single point of failure to a game. Distributed architectures eliminate these issues but add additional complexity in the synchronisation and robustness of the shared data. The work carried out by Cronin et al. [12] introduces an alternative synchronisation mechanism (called Trailing State Synchronisation) which offers a hybrid approach between the traditional client-server model and a distributed approach. It allows clients to share data in a peer to peer manner whilst periodically checking with the central server to confirm their state is correct. The results in this work appear promising but, in the worst case scenario, this system can result in multiple inconsistencies and delays due to the rollback mechanism.

Inconsistencies can manifest into flaws which can be exploited by users to create cheats for a game. By reducing the client side inconsistencies, these flaws can be prevented. However, maintaining consistency also means the restriction on the amount of data that a client can input into the game world or, at the very least, a hybrid design introducing a complex and inflexible protocol for game programmers to work around. Baughman et al. [13] proposed a protocol for multiplayer game communication that has anti-cheating guarantees. One particular module of the proposed Lockstep protocol works as a transaction based system, which has the guarantee that no host ever receives the state of another host before the game rules permit. This work then improves upon this relatively expensive new protocol with the author's faster Asynchronous Synchronization protocol, which relaxes the requirements of Lockstep by decentralizing the game clock. The results have suggested that cheating is effectively eliminated whilst also maintaining a good performance. However, in the examples demonstrated, integrating this technology into a project is non trivial and significant expertise will almost certainly be required.

We have previously undertaken research work in the similar area of multi-player synchronisation but with a very different approach to what we propose in this paper [14]. In order to create a protocol which reduces cheating, we proposed the idea of using a node based approach to lay out shared data in memory. Each of these nodes then had an owner attached and respective permissions. This allowed for a flexible protocol to be built, which was potentially trivial to maintain and extend. It also performed efficiently where players could interact with the world and make changes to any object or data they owned, whilst also preventing others from modifying unauthorised objects. Thus, this achieves protecting the server and other players from any potential cheating. The technology performed well and, as part of a prototype, was integrated with three existing games of an independent games development studio developed for LEGO. The fact that it could easily integrate with existing software, as opposed to software being built from scratch, demonstrated that this approach was very easy to maintain and extend.

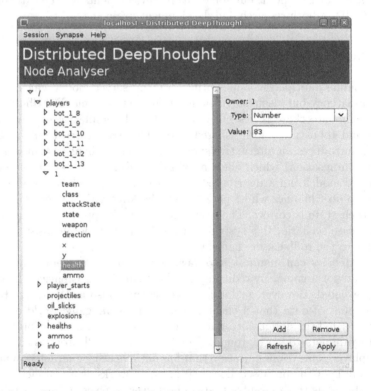

Fig. 1. A small internal tool which allowed for the debugging of the Distributed DeepThought node based hierarchy. This tool was invaluable in simulating and testing any potential damage that a malicious user could make.

However, we discovered a number of complexities with the protocol, described in Sect. 3, so our solution started to become hard to manage. The node ownership system works well for a number of scenarios but transferring ownership (i.e. as part of a trade) still felt overly complex. This very fact is what prompted us to look into new ways to reduce the need to synchronise the state entirely and move towards streaming technologies, such as the one we propose in this paper.

3   Complexities Involved in Client Synchronisation

Developing a multi user application is a more complicated and expensive process than single user software [15]. The main reason for this is because there are more entry points for the incorrect handling of data. Since there is effectively more than one unit of execution operating at a time, in a similar way to a multi-threaded application, it opens up the possibilities of race conditions and other time dependent bugs. This can cost time and effort to debug.

In a game scenario, for example, if a client opens up a door in the game world, the following steps need to follow:

1. The client notifies the server that they are attempting to open the door
2. The server decides whether they have the correct authorisation to do so
3. The server tells the client that the door is opened
4. The server then notifies all other clients that the door is open
5. The clients change the state in their copy of the game state so that the door is now open

With the increasingly complex network interactions evident in games today, including all the underlying data that need to be synchronised, it soon becomes evident that without an effective design, performing this process for similar events would quickly become unwieldy. This stands true especially if we now add the additional requirement that a new client is connecting and needs to be synchronised to the existing state on the server. The following steps would then be necessary:

1. A client connects to the server and requests a state synchronisation
2. The server needs to scan through its copy of the game state and serialize all the changeable states into a data stream and send to the client
3. The client receives this stream and processes it, updating and adding to its state as necessary
4. The server notifies all other clients that a new client has joined
5. Existing clients update their game state to include this new client

This synchronisation of data, depending on the size of the game world, could become very large and, without a good design, could potentially cause latency issues on other clients whilst the new client is being handled.

The next level of complexity is how clients interact with one another directly. For example, let us assume a scenario where they need to perform a trade of virtual items. Then, the following steps would need to be performed:

1. Client one informs the server they are trading an item with a specified ID with a client of specified ID
2. Client two informs the server they are trading their item with specified ID with a client of specified ID
3. Server matches the IDs to create an idea of a trade instance
4. Server checks that both items are valid and there is no cheating such as memory editing happening (see Sect. 4.4 for more details)
5. Server accepts the trade and sends success to each client
6. Each client now removes their traded item and creates a new object representing the item they received

The entire process provides a large number of potential entry points for bugs and synchronisation issues in the above scenarios. For example, let us assume that one of the clients disconnects at around step 4. Scanning the state and fixing failed trade instances could be one possible solution but this alone is a complex task. A suitably complex server could have many of these processes for a wide range of functionality which will all need care whilst implementing. Whilst this can certainly yield an acceptable and secure system, as seen in successful commercial games such as Quake 3, it still requires very experienced and disciplined programming [16]. However, the idea is that with a technology such as OpenGL|Distributed, all of these steps needed to synchronise client states can be avoided.

4   Inner Workings of OpenGL|D

OpenGL|D implements a client/server architecture where rather than having the running 3D program calling the OpenGL API to communicate with the GPU to rasterize a scene on the local machine, it, instead, creates a server for clients to connect to via a web browser. Once connected, the OpenGL calls are translated to a protocol and back to the client to finally be executed by the WebGL equivalents. Technically this creates a partition in the technology stack which is almost entirely independent from the hardware it runs on. This can be seen in Fig. 2. From a technical viewpoint this architecture has the benefit that complexity can be encapsulated. For example, results from memory checking tools such as Valgrind [17] can often be affected from details of the lower level layers of an operating system. With OpenGL|D, the boundary is limited to data being sent through a socket and, as such, the complex workings of the graphics driver stack can have no influence on the memory allocated by the program being tested.

From a digital preservation viewpoint, this architecture is useful because the 3D software can be run in a VM running an old operating system as a guest. The host can then run a web browser and simply connect to the server through the virtual machine boundary. However, from a multi-user collaboration viewpoint the additional benefit is that multiple clients can connect to this server and render out the same scene. This provides the foundation for OpenGL|D's use as a multi-user solution.

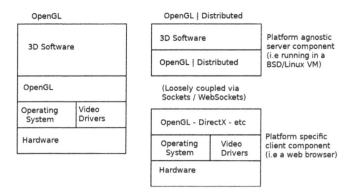

Fig. 2. Diagram describing the layers that OpenGL is built upon compared to OpenGL|D. Notice that OpenGL|D has additional layers of abstraction.

4.1 Protocol Overview

The OpenGL|D protocol is fairly straightforward. This is largely due to the fact that it can mimic how the computer's CPU and GPU communicate in a largely faithful manner. This also allows for traditional graphics programming optimisations to remain valid. When an OpenGL command is called, the server library encodes the command and data into a smaller message and forwards it onto the client. The client then decodes this message and executes it on the underlying platform, whether that is OpenGL, OpenGL|ES, WebGL or even other graphics APIs such as DirectX. Any necessary response is then sent back to the awaiting server. This is demonstrated in Fig. 3.

Due to the fact that OpenGL|D is designed to support a large number of connected clients, it is important that no specific operation blocks execution of the server whilst waiting for a response. This means that work undertaken to handle a client request must cause minimal delay for the other connected clients. In practice, this means that the example given in Fig. 3, which demonstrates synchronous requests, utilizes the OpenGL|D request buffer so that every message for that client after the required synchronous request is stored in a buffer, rather than executed until the dependent request is complete. It then processes the existing request buffer until it is empty or until another synchronous request is required. This works largely well and threads can be avoided which aids with portability. However, this architecture does increase memory usage. This may not be an issue when streaming graphics via OpenGL|D on a server but on a low-powered mobile device this becomes much more important if needing to stream to a large number of clients.

One important example of not blocking communication between clients is when the server handles a new client connection. The new client is updated with a snapshot of the entire current OpenGL state. Even though the state driven architecture of OpenGL works well here, there is still potentially a considerable amount of data to be sent, including textures, buffer objects, etc. However, a

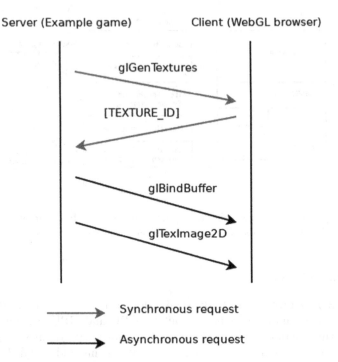

Fig. 3. Diagram demonstrating a typical yet simplified communication between the client and server components of OpenGL|D in order to upload a texture.

similar system to the one described previously is utilized. Whilst the client is being synchronised, new messages are stored in a buffer and processed when ready, whereas other clients remain unaffected (unless we run into bandwidth limitations). See Sect. 5.4 for an overview of planned optimization techniques.

4.2   How Clients Share a Single State

As described in the previous section, clients connect to a server and simply receive rendering commands whilst sending back key presses or mouse motion events. This means that clients themselves retain almost no state other than the OpenGL|D graphics state such as glEnable(), glEnableClientState() etc. This has the benefit of almost no complexity when syncing a new client. Once vertex buffers and textures are uploaded, the newly connected client is ready for future frames. If a potentially complex action occurs (as described earlier in the paper), such as opening a door or a trade, it happens only in one place, the server. Nothing will need to be synced to the clients to handle this event. They will receive their rendering commands as usual and continue. This behavior was demonstrated in a simple multiplayer football game (Fig. 4) where players would knock each other away from the ball whilst applying forces or "grabbing" the ball. Typically, this ownership of the ball would be complex to synchronise between

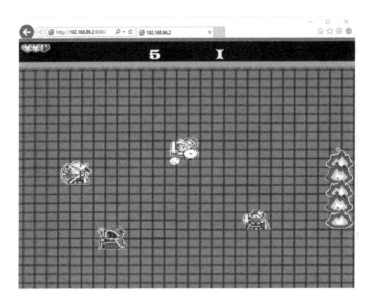

Fig. 4. Screenshot of Fantasy Football; a basic prototype multi-player football game demonstrating fast action and complex interaction between knocking other players away and "ownership" of the ball.

clients but, with OpenGL|D, this was not required at all. Applying forces between players can also be complex due to position snapshots often lagging behind in traditional synchronisation approaches. Again, with OpenGL|D, this complexity could be avoided.

4.3   Unique Client Specific Rendering

Other than perhaps some of the more basic collaboration software, it is important that even though clients share the same state with OpenGL|D, it is still possible for them to display different outputs. For example, in a 3D game, the clients would likely require a view of the game world from different camera angles, have different information on their heads up display (HUD) and perhaps even have GUI elements displayed just for them. This functionality is expressed very naturally with OpenGL|D in that whilst the update function is called just once per frame in OpenGL|D, the display callback is called multiple times for each connected client. This means that during the display function path, it is very easy to query which client ID is the current active one (via gldCurrentClientId()) and then either use the view matrix from its assigned camera to get a unique view port or go down a path of logic that displays the GUI for that client. The whole process could even be described akin to an extension to rendering to a texture, which is a common technique that developers have been using for years. A simple example can be seen in Fig. 5, where a player selection dialog is shown to a newly connected client without obstructing the view of existing players.

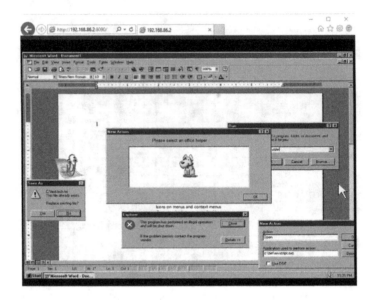

Fig. 5. Screenshot of Cloud Office 95; a basic prototype multi-player game developed during a games jam. One player has the character select menu open whereas it is hidden for other clients, demonstrating client specific rendering paths.

4.4 Cheat Prevention

Perhaps one of the more interesting features of using OpenGL|D as a solution for multi-user applications and games is that cheating can be eliminated. The clients themselves are akin to dumb terminals [18] and do no processing themselves. All they do is executing OpenGL commands and responding to key presses or mouse motion commands. This means that any modifications to the client cannot adversely affect the server because all it reads back from the client is a key press. The types of cheats this avoids include memory editors which can, among other things, freeze memory locations so data such as health cannot be decremented when a player is hurt. Other cheats involve the modification of the client and, if dealing with native C/C++ programs, entire functions dealing with player health could be patched out and replaced with null operations (NOPS) to, again, avoid the decreasing of values such as health. This is even more likely if a client is written in an interpreted language (such as Javascript) or JIT bytecode (i.e. JVM or .NET) since even if this is obfuscated, it is still relatively easy to patch or completely decompile these programs compared to native machine code.

5 Results and Discussion

5.1 Performance Evaluation

Compared to existing solutions involving manually syncing the client state [19, 20], there is virtually no network overhead when using OpenGL|D because, as discussed previously, there is no actual game state to synchronise. However, there certainly is a cost on bandwidth because we are effectively dealing with streaming technology and this means we must send enough data to generate a new image each frame. An additional overhead also needs to be considered when dealing with Websockets so that the output can be rendered in a web browser. Websockets have a much larger header than standard packets so require more data to be sent across the network. Websockets also do not support UDP technology so TCP is enforced even though, as with other streaming technology, the occasional dropped packet can be easily handled.

That said, compared to other streaming technology such as VNC which deals with rasterized images, OpenGL|D has the potential to be a much faster solution because it uses an intelligent protocol which sends the commands which can generate the output image on the destination hardware, rather than send over a pre-rendered image each frame. This can be seen in Fig. 6. If there are few models in the scene much less data needs to be transferred through to the client, whereas with VNC a map of the rasterized pixels is sent regardless. The bandwidth requirements when using OpenGL|D only start to match that of VNC when dealing with a large number of shapes (almost 10K). This is rarely the case in games due to optimization techniques used to reduce the number of draw calls.

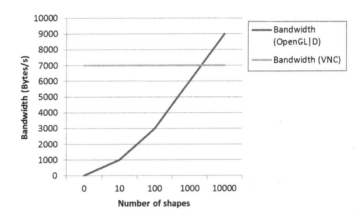

Fig. 6. Graph comparing the bandwidth requirements between OpenGL|D and VNC with a varying number of objects in the scene.

In general, network synchronisation via OpenGL|D will have the best performance compared to other solutions when only dealing with a small number of OpenGL draw calls and a large complex game state. Such examples could potentially include software with complex inventory systems that need to be interacted with via simple GUI systems in the client. It will also perform better than most rasterized streaming solutions at higher resolutions. OpenGL|D does

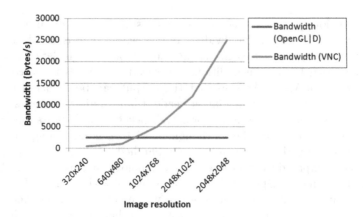

Fig. 7. Graph comparing the bandwidth requirements between OpenGL|D and VNC with an increasing image resolution.

not need to send through each pixel to the client, the clients do the actual rasterization, therefore there is no additional costs to bandwidth using OpenGL|D at higher resolutions. This is demonstrated in Fig. 7.

Network synchronisation via OpenGL|D will compare worse against other solutions when dealing with simple states to share (such as just synchronising projectiles and player positions) or large complex game worlds with many objects to render. Such examples could include real-time strategy (RTS) games or open world shooters.

5.2   Bandwidth Comparison with QuakeWorld

Whilst id's Quake is now regarded as a fairly antiquated game and certainly no longer cutting edge in any way, there have been a large number of improvements to its codebase (largely due to its open-source nature) such as FTE QuakeWorld which is still in active development [21]. The QuakeWorld client in particular still, in our view, provides an adequate test bed for comparison with OpenGL|D. What makes the QuakeWorld client very convenient to test against is that it employs an older implementation of OpenGL and so is fairly straightforward to port to using OpenGL|D. Whilst OpenGL|D does not yet provide a full coverage of an OpenGL API, the majority of functionality is there and, most importantly, the data is still being sent across the network so will still provide valid (albeit early) test results. One important limitation is that in our implementation, the different clients only see the same image rather than a unique image from their player's viewport. However, given the way that OpenGL|D works, this was deemed satisfactory and would not alter results in any way. Further work is certainly planned in this area.

Our initial tests agree with the work carried out by Cordeiro et al. [22] and Abdelkhalek et al. [23,24] and show that the QuakeWorld client has a generally low bandwidth requirement of 2–3 KB for both incoming and outgoing traffic.

This is with the official maximum of 32 players. However, this number does occasionally spike when an interesting event happens, such as a player death or teleportation. This suggests that the additional synchronisation messages required for such an event are in place and sent through the network so that the clients can keep up to date with the world state. In OpenGL|D it was predicted that these spikes would never exist. In the tests performed, whilst our prediction remained true, the base bandwidth required was consistently higher at around 6–7 KB. Again, this points to OpenGL|D's scalability being most effective in intricate and complex state updates rather than synchronising a large number of clients.

To demonstrate this view, a small modification (written in QuakeC) was made to the client to artificially produce a need for a large number of state changes. What this modification provided was the creation of a constant trade based system so that on each frame a virtual item was passed around the clients until one of the clients matched a set criteria. The additional bandwidth required for the locking and synchronisation involved in the trade of these items did start to increase. If around 50 of these trades happened at once, the bandwidth required matched that of the OpenGL|D client, whereas with the same trade mechanism, the OpenGL|D client showed no increase in bandwidth. Although rather artificial in nature, this very basic experiment demonstrates that for certain tasks, the synchronisation system provided by OpenGL|D can potentially scale in a more favorable way compared to traditional approaches.

5.3   Network Protocol Optimization Mirrors GPU

The overhead discussed previously can be greatly reduced using a variety of techniques. Most of these are techniques that are also evident in standard OpenGL software. In general, reducing the amount of data being sent to and from the graphics card translates almost exactly to reducing the amount of data being sent to and from the client and the server. A basic example is reducing the number of draw calls by batching mesh data together into vertex buffer objects (VBOs) and vertex array objects (VAOs). Grouping mesh data together based on material and texture can also avoid the need for binding a texture sampler between each mesh or changing light data.

Generally, once mesh and texture data has been uploaded to the client and the client state has been prepared, the only calls that need to be made are updating the model view matrix and initiating the drawing of a number of triangles (via glDrawArrays()). This means that much less data is sent through the network compared to other streaming technologies such as VNC. This is almost comparable to the manual synchronisation system found in existing games (yet retaining all the benefits of having a single program state).

5.4   Planned Optimisations

There are a number of optimization techniques we plan to introduce to OpenGL|D as and when required. The first priority is likely to be in the initial

Fig. 8. Screenshot of an example OpenGL|D output. An application with this rotating 3D model takes less than 10 bytes each frame. Even with maximum compression, VNC takes over 20 times that in bandwidth for a similar (but lower quality, lossy compressed) image.

synchronisation of the OpenGL state. In preliminary tests on mobile devices, we deemed it too expensive to compress every message before it is sent. However, as with most streaming technology the payload size sent for each frame is quite small anyway thus the effectiveness of most compression schemes is greatly reduced for this task. However, since the initial synchronisation of the client is likely to be much larger and can be delivered as a contiguous block of data, compression is likely to yield more positive results, making this a worthwhile avenue to explore for decreasing the initial load time.

The next priority is likely to lie in the sending of buffer objects and textures. Not only can these large blocks of data be compressed, but in the case of 2D textures, lossless encoding (such as with PNG) should produce even better results. Research into 3D image compression schemes will need to be undertaken in case sending an array of PNG images is suboptimal.

Finally, we realize that UDP is likely to be a more optimal solution than our existing TCP based system [25] and in the main draw routines, unreliable packet transmission can be handled effectively therefore, this faster but less reliable protocol is a feasible optimization. Only in transferring permanent state changes or uploading data objects is reliable transmission (either via TCP or a reliable UDP scheme) desired. However, our current priority is to support the transmission of data to a HTML5 web browser via WebSockets, which not only produce a larger overhead to raw sockets but also restrict our protocol to TCP based technology. In the future, if the web browser environment proves to be too volatile or too restrictive, a standalone OpenGL|D viewer is planned where the use of UDP can be explored in a more thorough fashion.

6 Summary of Discussion

The process of developing a multi-user project can be greatly simplified by using OpenGL|D. Not only is the developer released from the error-prone task of manually synchronising objects within the game but also new development architectures are made available. Rather than build up hierarchies of objects in a manner ready to be serialized and shared, the development process can now invest a greater focus on the logic to carry out tasks in a natural manner. A reduced number of callbacks and rules needs to be applied because the logic is effectively developed in exactly the same way as a single user experience. Arguably, this new flexibility in design also allows for greater support for logical distribution on clusters. This is because without needing to focus on the synchronisation of hierarchies between computers, this additional time can be spent solving the problems provided by traditional clustering complexities. The task of comparing OpenGL|D against VNC has been valuable. This is because in terms of portability, other solutions such as NoMachine's NX server [26] or GameStream [27], NVIDIA's commercial streaming technology, are not available on all but the most common platforms. This would greatly limit their ability to be used to facilitate digital preservation and perform on older platforms such as DOS or Plan 9 and newer platforms such as Tizen or Jolla/Sailfish. All of these platforms are supported by OpenGL|D and VNC however.

7 Conclusion and Future Work

Allowing users to share a single state provides some interesting avenues for analytical data. For example, most software will record an event when a specific action occurs. This happens in isolation from other users. However, if the same state is shared, it should be possible to obtain analytics data for choices the users have made at that exact second alongside one another. We can then compare the choices made knowing that all users have experienced exactly the same stimulus, distractions and context at the time the event triggered. This should ensure a more robust correlation between analytical results.

A future multi-user project involving OpenGL|D is a game to help learn and practice maths (Fig. 9). It is modeled after traditional light gun games such as House of the Dead or Time Crisis. Instead of aiming and pulling a trigger, a series of correct answers from the players will clear the enemies. With this in place, event data such as a user encountering a certain task and subsequently interacting and performing with it can be obtained and compared with the other players logged in at that time, dynamically changing the rules of the game. The main aim of this game is to encourage users to practice their maths by allowing them to play together which will result in repeat plays and thus hopefully increase the lifespan of the game itself. From a technical viewpoint, synchronising the

Fig. 9. Screenshot of the Zombie Maths Game. This early prototype has been trialled by a large number of participants and the results, which have been uploaded to our internal analytics server platform, have shown promise in terms of engagement and improvement for all age ranges.

enemies with maths questions on each client would potentially be non-trivial, however, OpenGL|D is very likely to simplify this process by virtue of each client implicitly sharing the same game state.

References

1. Pedersen, K., Gatzidis, C., Tang, W.: OpenGL|D - a multi-user single state architecture for multiplayer game development. In: International Conference on Cyberworlds 2017, Chester, UK, September 2017
2. Laurens, P., Paige, R.F., Brooke, P.J., Chivers, H.: A novel approach to the detection of cheating in multiplayer online games. In: 12th IEEE International Conference on Engineering Complex Computer Systems (ICECCS 2007), pp. 97–106, July 2007
3. Wu, D., Xue, Z., He, J.: icloudaccess: cost-effective streaming of video games from the cloud with low latency. IEEE Trans. Circuits Syst. Video Technol. **24**(8), 1405–1416 (2014)
4. Karachristos, T., Apostolatos, D., Metafas, D.: A real-time streaming games-on-demand system. In: Proceedings of the 3rd International Conference on Digital Interactive Media in Entertainment and Arts, DIMEA 2008, pp. 51–56. ACM, New York (2008). http://doi.acm.org/10.1145/1413634.1413648
5. Färber, J.: Traffic modelling for fast action network games. Multimedia Tools Appl. **23**(1), 31–46 (2004). http://dx.doi.org/10.1023/B:MTAP.0000026840.45588.64
6. Stagner, A.R.: Unity Multiplayer Games. Packt Publishing Ltd., Birmingham (2013)

7. Matthews, B., Shaon, A., Bicarregui, J., Jones, C.: A framework for software preservation. Int. J. Digit. Curation **5**(1), 91–105 (2010)
8. Microsoft, Introducing windows 10 s (2017). https://www.microsoft.com/en-us/windows/windows-10-s. Accessed 20 Jan 2017
9. Bassin, K., Santhanam, P.: Managing the maintenance of ported, outsourced, and legacy software via orthogonal defect classification. In: Proceedings of the IEEE International Conference on Software Maintenance, ICSM 2001, pp. 726–734 (2001)
10. Pellegrino, J.D., Dovrolis, C.: Bandwidth requirement and state consistency in three multiplayer game architectures. In: Proceedings of the 2nd Workshop on Network and System Support for Games, pp. 52–59. ACM (2003)
11. Wang, A.I., Jarrett, M., Sorteberg, E.: Experiences from implementing a mobile multiplayer real-time game for wireless networks with high latency. Int. J. Comput. Games Technol. **2009**, 6:1–6:14 (2009)
12. Cronin, E., Filstrup, B., Kurc, A.R., Jamin, S.: An efficient synchronization mechanism for mirrored game architectures. In: Proceedings of the 1st Workshop on Network and System Support for Games, pp. 67–73. ACM (2002)
13. Baughman, N.E., Levine, B.N.: Cheat-proof playout for centralized and distributed online games. In: Proceedings of the Twentieth Annual Joint Conference of the IEEE Computer and Communications Societies, IEEE INFOCOM 2001, vol. 1, pp. 104–113. IEEE (2001)
14. Pedersen, K., Gatzidis, C., Northern, B.: Distributed deepthought: synchronising complex network multi-player games in a scalable and flexible manner. In: Proceedings of the 3rd International Workshop on Games and Software Engineering: Engineering Computer Games to Enable Positive, Progressive Change, GAS 2013, pp. 40–43. IEEE Press, Piscataway (2013). http://dl.acm.org/citation.cfm?id=2662593.2662601
15. James, S.R., Gillam, B.D.: Network multiplayer game, 12 October 1999. US Patent 5,964,660
16. Sanglard, F.: Fabien sanglard's website (2012). http://fabiensanglard.net/quake3/network.php. Accessed 20 Jan 2017
17. Valgrind Developers: Valgrind memory debugger (2017). http://valgrind.org. Accessed 20 Jan 2017
18. Bulterman, D.C.A., van Liere, R.: Multimedia synchronization and UNIX. In: Herrtwich, R.G. (ed.) NOSSDAV 1991. LNCS, vol. 614, pp. 105–119. Springer, Heidelberg (1992). https://doi.org/10.1007/3-540-55639-7_10
19. Smed, J., Kaukoranta, T., Hakonen, H.: A review on networking and multiplayer computer games. Turku Centre for Computer Science (2002)
20. Smed, J., Kaukoranta, T., Hakonen, H.: Aspects of networking in multiplayer computer games. Electron. Libr. **20**(2), 87–97 (2002)
21. id Software: FTE quake world (2017). https://sourceforge.net/p/fteqw/code/HEAD/tree/trunk. Accessed 20 Oct 2017
22. Cordeiro, D., Goldman, A., da Silva, D.: Load balancing on an interactive multiplayer game server. In: Kermarrec, A.-M., Bougé, L., Priol, T. (eds.) Euro-Par 2007. LNCS, vol. 4641, pp. 184–194. Springer, Heidelberg (2007). https://doi.org/10.1007/978-3-540-74466-5_21
23. Abdelkhalek, A., Bilas, A., Moshovos, A.: Behavior and performance of interactive multi-player game servers. Cluster Comput. **6**(4), 355–366 (2003). https://doi.org/10.1023/A:1025718026938
24. Abdelkhalek, A., Bilas, A.: Parallelization and performance of interactive multiplayer game servers. In: Proceedings of the 18th International Parallel and Distributed Processing Symposium, pp. 7–8, April 2004

25. Xylomenos, G., Polyzos, G.C.: TCP and UDP performance over a wireless LAN. In: Proceedings of the Eighteenth Annual Joint Conference of the IEEE Computer and Communications Societies, IEEE INFOCOM 1999, vol. 2, pp. 439–446, March 1999
26. NoMachine, Nomachine NX server (2017). http://www.nomachine.com. Accessed 20 Jan 2017
27. NVIDIA: NVIDIA gamestream: Play PC games on NVIDIA shield (2017). http://www.nvidia.co.uk/shield/games/gamestream. Accessed 20 Jan 2017

Image Quality-Based
Illumination-Invariant Face Recognition

Fatema Tuz Zohra$^{(\boxtimes)}$ and Marina Gavrilova

Department of Computer Science, Faculty of Science, University of Calgary,
2500 University Drive N.W., Calgary, AB T2N 1N4, Canada
{fatematuz.zohra,mgavrilo}@ucalgary.ca

Abstract. Quality of biometric samples has a significant impact on the accuracy of a biometric recognition system. Various quality factors, such as different lighting conditions, occlusion, and variations in pose and expression may affect an automated face recognition system. One of the most challenging issues in automated face recognition is intra-class variations introduced by the varied facial quality due to the variation in illumination conditions. In this paper, we proposed an adaptive discrete wavelet transform (DWT) based face recognition approach which will normalize the illumination distortion using quality-based normalization approaches. The DWT based approach is used to extract the low and high frequency sub-bands for representing the facial features. In the proposed method, a weighted fusion of the low and high frequency sub-bands is computed to improve the identification accuracy under varying lighting conditions. The selection of fusion parameters is made using fuzzy membership functions. The performance of the proposed method was validated on the Extended Yale Database B. Experimental result shows that the proposed method outperforms some well-known face recognition approaches.

Keywords: Facial recognition · Biometric image quality
Discrete wavelet transform (DWT) · Adaptive quality · Fuzzy weights

1 Introduction

Automatic face recognition technology has reached a certain maturity level over the past decade. Continued development in this field introduces many benchmark face recognition approaches that can efficiently and reliably recognize faces under controlled environment. However, most of these approaches will result in degraded recognition performance while handling poor quality of data due to changes in lighting conditions, facial expressions, pose, occlusion, and poor sensor quality [1,7,14,19,30]. Degradation in these facial quality issues introduces intra-class variations which lead to higher identification errors in the systems. Variation in illumination conditions is one of the most challenging quality issues that significantly deteriorate the recognition performance, and that need to be

© Springer-Verlag GmbH Germany, part of Springer Nature 2018
M. L. Gavrilova et al. (Eds.): Trans. on Comput. Sci. XXXII, LNCS 10830, pp. 75–89, 2018.
https://doi.org/10.1007/978-3-662-56672-5_6

handled efficiently [10, 25, 29]. Another challenging issue for face recognition is the collection of adequate samples per person for recognizing faces in a real life scenario. Therefore, an adaptive face recognition system is needed that will handle the varying lighting conditions based on the illumination quality factors with a small number of training samples.

Wavelet based face recognition approaches are popular for developing illumination and expression invariant face recognition [5, 8]. Discrete wavelet transforms (DWTs) is an image analysis tool that decomposes the low and high frequency sub-bands at different scales. Authors in [23, 24] showed that low frequency sub-bands (LL) from the DWT can be used as an efficient face descriptor under controlled environment. However, the low frequency sub-bands are severely sensitive to illumination variations. On the other hand, the high frequency sub-bands perform well under varying illumination conditions due to the presence of less image details. Therefore, an adaptive fusion of the low and high frequency sub-bands is needed based on the degree of illumination distortion of the probe image for improving the recognition performance under varying illumination conditions. In this paper, we propose an adaptive face recognition system that will minimize the adverse impact of different quality factors by using a wavelet based approach. In this method, a score level weighted fusion of the low and high frequency sub-bands is applied to get the optimum results using illumination quality. This article is the extended version of the research paper presented in Cyberworlds 2017 by Zohra et al. [31]. The contribution of this revised manuscript is twofold:

1. An illumination normalization approach based on contrast limited adaptive histogram equalization (CLAHE) and DCT-based normalization is proposed to minimize the illumination distortion.
2. A weighted fusion of low and high frequency sub-bands from discrete wavelet transform is introduced to compute the identification accuracy. Fuzzy membership functions are used to calculate the fusion parameters based on the illumination quality [18, 27].

The organization of the rest of the paper is as follows: Sect. 2 presents a comprehensive study of the existing illumination invariant face recognition approaches in the literature. The detailed description of the proposed adaptive illumination-invariant face recognition approach is presented in Sect. 3. The evaluation database, experimental setup and results are discussed in Sect. 4. Finally, Sect. 5 summarizes the discussion.

2   Literature Review

One of the most challenging problems in face recognition is the intra-class variation introduced by varying illumination conditions at the identification and enrollment stages. The performance of most of the benchmark face recognition approaches is highly sensitive to the deviation of the quality of the facial samples due to the illumination changes. The most common approaches employed to solve variability in image illumination include the use of illumination invariant face descriptors [12,17,20,24], application of illumination normalization methods [6,10,15,26], and 3D modelling of faces [3,4,11,13].

Use of illumination invariant face descriptors is one of the common approaches to address the illumination variation problems. Illumination invariant face descriptors, such as Edge maps [12], Gabor wavelets [20], DWT [23,24] and DTCWT [17] have been proposed in the literature to deal with illumination changes. However, these approaches fail in case of extremely poor lighting conditions and changes of lighting directions. In addition, the performance of these face descriptors highly depends on the degree of lighting variance. Another approach is to use illumination normalization methods to address the varying illumination condition problems. Some of the well-known normalization techniques are histogram equalization [15], histogram matching and gamma intensity correction. Recently, more advance normalization techniques, such as DCT based normalization [6] and wavelet based normalization techniques [9,10] are being used to minimize the adverse effects of illumination variations. However, authors in [25], showed that global application of illumination normalization methods without considering the degree of illumination changes may degrade the illumination quality of well-lit facial images. A region-based illumination normalization approach was proposed in [26], where the facial sample was divided into regions, and illumination normalization method was applied separately for each region. The region-based method performs well compared to the traditional global normalization approaches.

Another set of approaches that is used to eliminate the effect of illumination variations includes 3D modeling of face variations. In this approach, a 3-D face model is constructed to consider the face images with different poses under varying lighting conditions [3,4,11,13]. A low dimension illumination space representation was proposed in [13], where the illumination space is constructed using 9 basis images under 9 different light sources. Authors in [4,11] presented a generative model called illumination cone or convex cone, which is mainly a set of images of an object under fixed pose and all possible illumination conditions. The method proposed in [3] indicates that a set of images of a complex Lambertian object under a wide range of lighting conditions can be accurately approximated by a 9D linear subspace. The main drawback of these approaches is that they require an adequate number of training samples under as many lighting variations as possible, or 3D shape information to represent faces in the illumination space.

In recent years, wavelet based face recognition approaches are gaining popularity for solving the intra-class variation problem introduced by varying illumination conditions [5,8,24,25]. The low and high frequency sub-bands extracted from wavelet transform of the facial images can be used as a facial descriptor for the recognition purpose. Typically, the low frequency sub-bands contain the most discriminating features of faces. However, they are very sensitive to illumination changes. On the contrary, high frequency sub-bands contain less image details, as a result they are less susceptible to varying lighting conditions.

Authors in [8,22] used wavelet based approaches for reducing the image dimensionality prior to the recognition process. A discrete wavelet transform (DWT) based face recognition approach was presented in [25], where a regional image enhancement technique was applied based on the illumination quality. However, this approach suffers from a sharp boundary problem as the threshold for selecting bad quality images and the fusion parameters are predefined. Another regional image enhancement technique based on DWT was proposed in [10]. In this method, the facial image was segmented into regions based on the degree of illumination. The authors applied a region based image enhancement technique to enlarge the edges from the high frequency features. The main drawback of this approach is that the performance of the method depends on the block size.

Illumination invariant face recognition approaches are thus required to fill the gap between finding an appropriate image quality based illumination normalization process, and an efficient face descriptor to determine the recognition performance from the normalized images. While developing an illumination invariant system, it is important to consider the degree of illumination distortion, as the performance of the recognition systems can be heavily affected by the uncertain degradation of samples due to extreme illumination distortion. Therefore, we propose an adaptive face recognition system based on image quality which will compensate for different lighting conditions by using appropriate face descriptor and normalization approaches. The proposed adaptive illumination-invariant approach is presented below.

3   Image Quality Based Adaptive Face Recognition

In biometric, quality of sample significantly affects the recognition or identification rate of the system. Image quality attributes such as contrast, brightness, sharpness, focus and illumination can be defined as the facial quality factors, as variation of these attributes has an impact on the performance of the system [1,30]. Therefore, an adaptive system is needed, to consider the quality factors, and to handle the quality issues based on the quality measures. In this paper, we propose an adaptive face recognition system based on the weighted score fusion of multiple sub-bands using Discrete Wavelet Transform (DWT). The input images are normalized using contrast limited adaptive histogram equalization (CLAHE) and discrete cosine transform (DCT) based normalization. After that, the low frequency sub-bands (LL) and high frequency sub-bands (LH and HL) from the 2nd level wavelet decomposition are fused together at the score level to recognize the faces. Fuzzy weights are calculated based on the quality measures using fuzzy membership functions to adaptively fuse the scores from different sub-bands. The proposed method consists of three modules, namely (i) quality measure, (ii) adaptive illumination normalization, and (iii) DWT based weighted score fusion. A block diagram of the proposed method is shown in Fig. 1. The following subsections present a detailed description of the method.

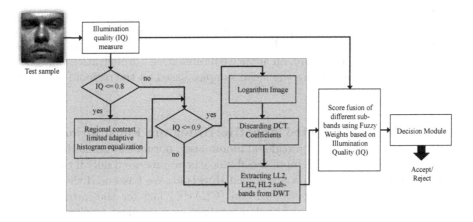

Fig. 1. Block diagram of the proposed method.

3.1 Quality Measure

The facial quality factors can be categorized based on digital formatting of facial images, scenes and photographs. The frequently used quality factors are: (a) brightness, (b) contrast, (c) focus, (d) illumination, (e) pose variations, and (f) occlusion [1,7,21,25]. In this paper, we are interested in estimating the illumination score.

Illumination: In most of the face biometric system, the enrolled or template facial images are taken under uniform lighting conditions. However, this is not the case for the test samples. The test samples can be obtained from an uncontrolled environment, having uncertain illumination conditions. For the proposed method, the illumination quality (IQ) is calculated by determining the luminance distortion between the reference image and the test sample. The reference image is the average of all the template images for the recognition system. The luminance distortion between two images x and y can be determined using Eq. 1 obtained from the Universal Quality Index (UQI) proposed in [29]. Equation 2 defines $\bar{x}$ and $\bar{y}$ that is the average intensity of the reference image and the probe image. The illumination quality score ranges from 0 to 1.

$$I = \frac{2\bar{x}\bar{y}}{(\bar{x})^2 + (\bar{y})^2} \tag{1}$$

$$\bar{x} = \frac{1}{N}\sum_{i=1}^{N} x_i, \quad \bar{y} = \frac{1}{N}\sum_{i=1}^{N} y_i \tag{2}$$

3.2 Adaptive Illumination Normalization

The most common approach for illumination normalization is to preprocess the biometric samples using normalization techniques, such as histogram equalization (HE), histogram matching, contrast limited adaptive histogram equalization

(CLAHE), and gamma intensity correction. However, quality enhancement using illumination normalization depends on the degree of illumination variance [25]. Moreover, the facial images can be affected with regional variation in illumination quality [25,26]. Therefore, an adaptive illumination normalization approach is needed that will preprocess the facial samples based on the regional illumination variance.

Regional Contrast Limited Adaptive Histogram Equalization: In the proposed method, we adopt a regional illumination normalization method based on illumination quality. The input facial image is preprocessed only if the illumination quality is lower than a predefined threshold. We have used the contrast limited adaptive histogram equalization (CLAHE) [32] for the normalization process. The regional quality based normalization is applied to those regions where the regional quality score is lower than a predefined threshold. In this way, we ensure that the good quality samples are unaffected from the normalization process, and normalization is applied to only the bad quality samples. Figure 2 shows example facial images before and after regional contrast limited adaptive histogram equalization. Figure 2(a), (c), and (e) are the original facial images. They show the global and regional illumination quality scores before

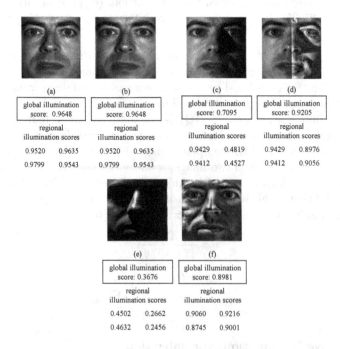

Fig. 2. Example of facial images before and after the regional contrast limited adaptive histogram equalization. (a), (c), and (e) are the input facial images, and (b), (d), and (f) are the output facial images after the normalization process.

the normalization process. Figure 2(b), (d), and (f) are the output facial images after the normalization process. From the figure, it is clear that the normalization process improves the global and regional illumination quality scores.

Illumination Normalization in the DCT Domain: In [6], authors proposed DCT-based technique for illumination normalization. In this normalization process, low-frequency DCT coefficients are discarded as they are highly related to illumination changes. The proposed method uses DCT-based normalization to enhance the image quality. The facial image after the regional illumination normalization is transformed in the logarithmic domain. After that, this logarithm image is converted into the DCT domain to get the DCT coefficients. The 2D DCT for an input image A of size $M \times N$ can be defined using Eq. 3 [6]. Here, the values B_{pq} is called the DCT coefficients of A.

$$
B_{pq} = \alpha_p \alpha_q \sum_{m=0}^{M-1} \sum_{n=0}^{N-1} A_{mn}
$$
$$
\times \cos\left[\frac{\pi(2m+1)p}{2M}\right] \cos\left[\frac{\pi(2n+1)q}{2N}\right] \tag{3}
$$

where $0 \le p \le M - 1$ and $0 \le q \le N - 1$, and

$$
\alpha_p = \begin{cases} \frac{1}{\sqrt{M}}, & p = 0 \\ \frac{2}{\sqrt{M}}, & p = 1, 2, ..., M - 1 \end{cases}
$$

$$
\alpha_q = \begin{cases} \frac{1}{\sqrt{N}}, & q = 0 \\ \frac{2}{\sqrt{N}}, & q = 1, 2, ..., N - 1 \end{cases}
$$

3.3 DWT Based Weighted Score Fusion for Face Recognition

Discrete wavelet transform (DWT) is a signal or image processing tool that segments the signal or image into low and high frequency sub-bands at different scales. Authors in [23,24] showed that low frequency sub-bands (LL) from the DWT can be used as an efficient face descriptor for the facial images captured under ideal conditions. However, the effectiveness of this method will be lost under varying illumination condition of the facial images. This is because the low frequency sub-bands contain the most prominent facial features, but they are severely sensitive to illumination variations. On the other hand, the high frequency sub-bands (e.g. the horizontal (HL) and vertical (LH) features) perform relatively well under varying illumination changes, but they are sensitive to expression and pose changes. In the presence of various lighting conditions, the individual scores from the low or high frequency sub-bands may not produce optimum results for the face recognition. Therefore, an adaptive fusion of the low and high frequency sub-bands based on the degree of illumination changes of the probe image is needed, which can improve the recognition performance under varying illumination conditions.

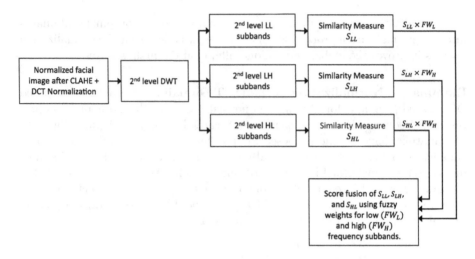

Fig. 3. Block diagram of the score level fusion of low and high frequency DWT sub-bands using quality based fuzzy weights.

DWT-Based Face Recognition: In this paper, we propose a score level fusion of the low and high frequency sub-bands to get the optimum results. In the proposed method, 2D DWT is applied on face images of size 128×128. We have empirically found that the second level DWT sub-bands performs well under varying lighting conditions for the face recognition. Therefore, the input image is decomposed up to the 2nd level to obtain the LL2, HL2, LH2 sub-bands. These subband coefficients are normalized using Z-score normalization (ZN) to improve the identification accuracy. Similarity scores for each subband (LL2, HL2, and LH2) are calculated by comparing the template and the probe images. These similarity scores are then fused by determining the weighted average of the scores. The fusion parameters have a significant impact on the recognition rate. Therefore, we propose an adaptive approach to calculate the fusion weights using fuzzy membership functions based on the illumination quality of the probe image.

Quality Based Fuzzy Weights for Score Fusion: Predefined fusion parameters will not be able to cope with the changing lighting conditions. We need to assign appropriate weights for fusing the scores which will result in optimum results for the face recognition. Therefore, the fusion parameters are set adaptively based on the illumination quality (IQ). If the quality score is lower than a predefined threshold, then the low and high frequency sub-bands are fused, otherwise only the low frequency features are considered for the identification purpose. Two fuzzy weights (FW_L and FW_H) respectively, for the low and high frequency sub-bands are calculated using sigmoid and z-shape fuzzy membership functions [27]. Equations 4 and 5 describe the Sigmoidal and Z-shaped fuzzy membership functions for calculating $(FW_L$ and $FW_H)$.

$$FW_L(IQ) = \frac{1}{1 + e^{-a(IQ-b)}} \tag{4}$$

$$FW_H(IQ) = \begin{cases} 1, & IQ \leq c \\ 1 - 2\left(\frac{IQ-c}{c-d}\right)^2, & c \leq IQ \leq \frac{c+d}{2} \\ 2\left(\frac{IQ-d}{d-c}\right)^2, & \frac{c+d}{2} \leq IQ \leq d \\ 0, & IQ \leq d \end{cases} \tag{5}$$

Here, IQ is the illumination quality score of the probe image, and a, b, c and d are threshold values for the Sigmoidal and Z-shaped membership functions. The values of a, b, c and d should be real numbers, with $c < d$. We have empirically selected the optimal values for a, b, c and d. For the proposed method the values of these thresholds are set to $a = 0.3$, $b = 0.6$, $c = 0.6$, and $d = 1.1$. Figure 3 depicts the score level fusion of the DWT sub-bands using fuzzy membership functions.

4   Experimental Results

4.1   Evaluation Data and Experimental Setup

For the validation of the proposed method, we consider the Extended Yale database B [11,16]. The database consists of 38 subject images under 64 different lighting conditions. These image samples from the database are divided into five illumination sets according to the angle θ [11,16]. Here, θ represents the light source with respect to the optical axis of the camera. Set 1 to set 5 have the illumination degradations in ascending order. Samples captured with frontal pose and under direct illumination (i.e., P00A+000E+00 image of each subject) are considered for training purpose. The original images of size 168×192 are resampled to a fixed size of 128×128. Figure 4 depicts the example images from five different illumination sets according to θ. We have conducted extensive experiments to validate the proposed method.

4.2   Results and Discussion

Initially, we have accomplished some experiments to find the optimal level of decomposition for the low and high frequency sub-bands for recognizing the faces. Table 1 shows the recognition rates (%) for low and high frequency sub-bands at different scales. We have decomposed the input up to 3rd level DWT, and the recognition rates for LL1, LL2, LL3, LH1, LH2, LH3, HL1, HL2, and HL3 sub-bands are shown in the Table 1. From the table, it is clear that low frequency sub-bands perform well for the well lit facial images. However, the recognition rate with low frequency sub-bands degrades rapidly with the degree of illumination distortion. On the other hand, high frequency sub-bands perform

Number of images	Light Source angle	Sample Images

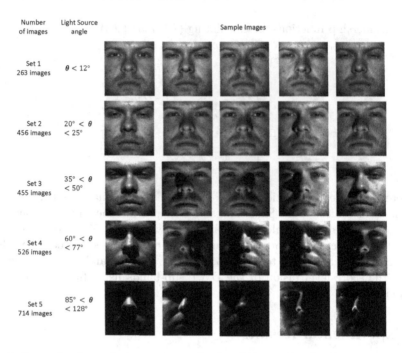

Fig. 4. Example of sample images from the five different illumination sets according to the angle θ.

better than the low frequency sub-bands for highly distorted facial images. Also, from the table, we can observe that the low and high frequency sub-bands at level 2 performs better than the frequency sub-bands at other levels. However, the recognition rate for the samples of set 4 and 5 is relatively low for both the

Table 1. Recognition performance (%) of the five illumination sets using low and high frequency sub-bands at different scales.

Wavelet subbands	Recognition rate (%)				
	Set 1	Set 2	Set 3	Set 4	Set 5
LL1	99.24	100	81.53	45.81	42.29
LH1	80.98	97.80	74.28	68.25	39.91
HL1	81.36	100	78.46	80.98	79.41
LL2	99.62	100	80	41.25	35.85
LH2	87.45	99.12	79.12	70.3	39.35
HL2	88.59	100	81.31	82.13	83.89
LL3	99.24	100	72.52	31.17	25.91
LH3	93.91	100	84.39	41.25	23.24
HL3	92.39	98.90	73.84	59.88	69.18

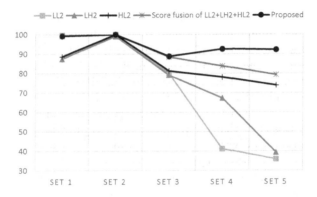

Fig. 5. Comparison of the recognition rate (%) for 5 different illumination sets under degrading lighting conditions using different sub-bands and fusion of the sub-bands.

low and high frequency sub-bands. Therefore, we have computed the weighted fusion of the three sub-bands LL2, LH2 and HL2 using the fuzzy membership functions. Figure 5 presents the recognition rate for all the five illumination sets using LL2, LH2, HL2 frequency sub-bands. It also shows the recognition rate using the weighted fusion of the three sub-bands and the recognition rate of our proposed method. From the figure, it is clear that the proposed method performs better than the other approaches.

Next, we have done some experiments on the impact of the illumination normalization process. Figure 6 shows the recognition rate (%) using a bar chart for the five different illumination sets. From this figure, we can see that when we have applied illumination normalization using regional contrast limited adaptive histogram equalization (CLAHE) and DCT based normalization, the recognition rate is higher than that for the methods with no illumination normalization or

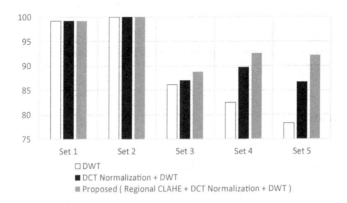

Fig. 6. Comparison of the recognition rate (%) for 5 different illumination sets using different illumination normalization process.

methods with different illumination normalization process. The proposed method using quality-based illumination normalization significantly improves the recognition rate for the samples with high illumination distortions (set 3, 4 and 5).

We have evaluated the performance of our proposed method with some state of the art face recognition approaches, such as Eigenface [28], Local Binary Pattern [2], DCT [6] and DWT [8] on the Extended Yale Database B. The recognition rate (%) for all these methods and the proposed method is shown in Fig. 7. From the figure, it is clear that the proposed method provides consistent results for the illumination sets with degrading lighting conditions. The well known Eigenface approach for face recognition obtains very poor results for all of the sets because of the single sample problem. The LBP based face recognition performs well for the well lit images, but the recognition rate degrades significantly with the extent of the illumination distortion. Similarly, the recognition rate for the DCT and DWT based face recognition shows similar pattern as the LBP based method. On the other hand, the proposed method outperforms all these face recognition approaches. Also, the proposed approach is less sensitive to the illumination changes, that is the rate of degradation of the recognition rate is much lower than that for the state of the art face recognition approaches for the samples with extreme illumination distortion.

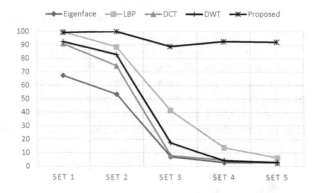

Fig. 7. Performance comparison of state of the art face recognition approaches with the proposed approach.

5 Conclusion

In this paper, we developed an image quality based adaptive face recognition system. We addressed the problem of face recognition under varying illumination conditions where there is only one sample available for the training purposes. A DWT based face recognition system is proposed using a weighted fusion of the low and high frequency sub-bands. The weight values for fusing the sub-bands are calculated using fuzzy membership functions based on the illumination quality of the sample image. Also, we have applied regional contrast limited adaptive histogram equalization (CLAHE) and DCT based normalization to minimize the impact of illumination changes. Experimental results show that the proposed method outperforms state of the art face recognition methods under varying lighting conditions. In the future, we will focus on designing a more powerful adaptive system that will consider other facial qualities, such as contrast, brightness, occlusion, pose and expression variations.

Acknowledgment. We would like to acknowledge NSERC Discovery Grant RT731064, as well as NSERC ENGAGE and URGC for partial funding of this project. Our thanks to all the members of BTLab, Department of Computer Science, University of Calgary, Calgary, AB, Canada for providing their valuable suggestions and feedback.

References

1. Abaza, A., Harrison, M.A., Bourlai, T., Ross, A.: Design and evaluation of photometric image quality measures for effective face recognition. IET Biom. **3**(4), 314–324 (2014)
2. Ahonen, T., Hadid, A., Pietikainen, M.: Face description with local binary patterns: application to face recognition. IEEE Trans. Pattern Anal. Mach. Intell. **28**(12), 2037–2041 (2006)
3. Basri, R., Jacobs, D.W.: Lambertian reflectance and linear subspaces. IEEE Trans. Pattern Anal. Mach. Intell. **25**(2), 218–233 (2003)
4. Belhumeur, P.N., Kriegman, D.J.: What is the set of image of and object under all possible lighting conditions. In: Proceedings of IEEE Computer Vision and Pattern Recognition, pp. 270–277 (1996)
5. Cao, X., Shen, W., Yu, L.G., Wang, Y.L., Yang, J.Y., Zhang, Z.W.: Illumination invariant extraction for face recognition using neighboring wavelet coefficients. Pattern Recogn. **45**(4), 1299–1305 (2012)
6. Chen, W., Er, M.J., Wu, S.: Illumination compensation and normalization for robust face recognition using discrete cosine transform in logarithm domain. IEEE Trans. Syst. Man Cybern. Part B (Cybern.) **36**(2), 458–466 (2006)
7. Chen, J., Deng, Y., Bai, G., Su, G.: Face image quality assessment based on learning to rank. IEEE Sig. Process. Lett. **22**(1), 90–94 (2015)
8. Chien, J.T., Wu, C.C.: Discriminant waveletfaces and nearest feature classifiers for face recognition. IEEE Trans. Pattern Anal. Mach. Intell. **24**(12), 1644–1649 (2002)
9. Du, S., Ward, R.: Wavelet-based illumination normalization for face recognition. In: IEEE International Conference on Image Processing, ICIP, vol. 2, pp. II–954. IEEE, September 2005
10. Du, S., Ward, R.K.: Adaptive region-based image enhancement method for robust face recognition under variable illumination conditions. IEEE Trans. Circ. Syst. Video Technol. **20**(9), 1165–1175 (2010)
11. Georghiades, A.S., Belhumeur, P.N., Kriegman, D.J.: From few to many: illumination cone models for face recognition under variable lighting and pose. IEEE Trans. Pattern Anal. Mach. Intell. **23**(6), 643–660 (2001)
12. Govindaraju, V., Sher, D.B., Srihari, R.K., Srihari, S.N.: Locating human faces in newspaper photographs. In: Proceedings of IEEE Computer Society Conference on Computer Vision and Pattern Recognition, CVPR 1989, pp. 549–554. IEEE, June 1989

13. Hallinan, P.W.: A low-dimensional representation of human faces for arbitrary lighting conditions. In: Proceedings of IEEE Conference on Computer Vision and Pattern Recognition, CVPR, Seattle, WA, vol. 94, pp. 995–999, June 1994

14. Li, S.Z., Jain, A.K.: Handbook of Face Recognition. Springer, New York (2011). https://doi.org/10.1007/978-0-85729-932-1

15. Kim, Y.T.: Contrast enhancement using brightness preserving bi-histogram equalization. IEEE Trans. Consum. Electron. **43**(1), 1–8 (1997)

16. Lee, K.C., Ho, J., Kriegman, D.J.: Acquiring linear subspaces for face recognition under variable lighting. IEEE Trans. Pattern Ana. Mach. Intell. **27**(5), 684–698 (2005)

17. Liu, C.C., Dai, D.Q.: Face recognition using dual-tree complex wavelet features. IEEE Trans. Image Process. **18**(11), 2593–2599 (2009)

18. Monwar, M.M., Gavrilova, M., Wang, Y.: A novel fuzzy multimodal information fusion technology for human biometric traits identification. In: 10th IEEE International Conference on Cognitive Informatics and Cognitive Computing (ICCI* CC), pp. 112–119. IEEE, August 2011

19. Punnappurath, A., Rajagopalan, A.N., Taheri, S., Chellappa, R., Seetharaman, G.: Face recognition across non-uniform motion blur, illumination, and pose. IEEE Trans. Image Process. **24**(7), 2067–2082 (2015)

20. Qing, L., Shan, S., Chen, X., Gao, W.: Face recognition under varying lighting based on the probabilistic model of Gabor phase. In: 18th International Conference on Pattern Recognition, ICPR, vol. 3, pp. 1139–1142. IEEE, August 2006

21. Sang, J., Lei, Z., Li, S.Z.: Face image quality evaluation for ISO/IEC standards 19794-5 and 29794-5. In: Tistarelli, M., Nixon, M.S. (eds.) ICB 2009. LNCS, vol. 5558, pp. 229–238. Springer, Heidelberg (2009). https://doi.org/10.1007/978-3-642-01793-3_24

22. Sellahewa, H., Jassim, S.A.: Wavelet-based face verification for constrained platforms. In: Proceedings of SPIE Biometric Technology for Human Identification II, vol. 5779, pp. 173–183, March 2005

23. Sellahewa, H.: Wavelet based automatic face recognition for constrained devices. Ph.D. dissertation, University of Buckingham (2006)

24. Sellahewa, H., Jassim, S.A.: Illumination and expression invariant face recognition: toward sample quality-based adaptive fusion. In: 2nd IEEE International Conference on Biometrics: Theory, Applications and Systems, BTAS, pp. 1–6. IEEE, September 2008

25. Sellahewa, H., Jassim, S.A.: Image-quality-based adaptive face recognition. IEEE Trans. Instrum. Meas. **59**(4), 805–813 (2010)

26. Shan, S., Gao, W., Cao, B., Zhao, D.: Illumination normalization for robust face recognition against varying lighting conditions. In: IEEE International Workshop on Analysis and Modeling of Faces and Gestures, AMFG, pp. 157–164. IEEE, October 2003

27. Sultana, M., Gavrilova, M., Alhajj, R., Yanushkevich, S.: Adaptive multi-stream score fusion for illumination invariant face recognition. In: IEEE Symposium on Computational Intelligence in Biometrics and Identity Management (CIBIM), pp. 94–101. IEEE, December 2014

28. Turk, M., Pentland, A.: Eigenfaces for recognition. J. Cogn. Neurosci. **3**(1), 71–86 (1991)

29. Wang, Z., Bovik, A.C.: A universal image quality index. IEEE Sig. Process. Lett. **9**(3), 81–84 (2002)

30. Zohra, F.T., Rahman, M.W., Gavrilova, M.: Occlusion detection and localization from Kinect depth images. In: International Conference on Cyberworlds (CW), pp. 189–196. IEEE, September 2016
31. Zohra, F.T., Gavrilova, M.: Adaptive face recognition based on image quality. In: International Conference on Cyberworlds (CW). IEEE (2017)
32. Zuiderveld, K.: Contrast limited adaptive histogram equalization. In: Heckbert, P.S. (ed.) Graphics Gems IV, pp. 474–485. Academic Press Professional Inc., San Diego (1994)

Synthesizing Imagined Faces
Based on Relevance Feedback

Caie Xu[1], Shota Fushimi[1], Masahiro Toyoura[1], Jiayi Xu[2],
and Xiaoyang Mao[1(✉)]

[1] University of Yamanashi, Yamanashi, Japan
mao@yamanashi.ac.jp
[2] Hangzhou Dianzi University, Hangzhou, China

Abstract. In this paper, we propose a user-friendly system that can create a
facial image from a corresponding image in the user's mind. Unlike most of the
existing methods, which require a sketch as input or the tedious work of
selecting similar facial components from an example database, our method can
synthesise a satisfying result without questioning the user on the explicit features of the face in his or her mind. Through a dialogic approach based on a
relevance feedback strategy to translate facial features into input, the user only
needs to look at several candidate face images and judge whether each image
resembles the face that he or she is imagining. A set of sample face images that
are based on users' feedbacks are used to dynamically train an Optimum-Path
Forest algorithm to classify the relevance of face images. Based on the trained
Optimum-Path Forest classifier, candidate face images that best reflect the user's
feedback are retrieved and interpolated to synthesise new face images that are
similar to those the user had imagined. The experimental results show that the
proposed technique succeeded in generating images resembling a face a user had
imagined or memorised.

Keywords: Face image synthesis · Relevance feedback · Optimum-Path Forest

1 Introduction

Face image synthesis has potential applications in public safety, such as video
surveillance and law enforcement. For example, creating a portrait of a suspect from an
eyewitness can greatly help the police identify criminals. Also, a similar technique can
be used for giving concrete form to imagined ideas of romantic 'types' and translate
other imagined faces into explicit images. However, drawing an image based on
descriptions of what is in one's mind is not an easy task for the majority of people.
Although the montage approach to face image synthesis [1] allows users to create face
images by selecting face components, it involves the time-consuming task of choosing
the right parts from a wide array of options. It is known that the composition of face parts
is a more important factor in the perception of a face than the individual parts [2].
However, it can be very difficult to adjust the positions of individual parts to achieve a
desired composition. Several methods have been developed for synthesising face
images according to sketches [3]. Such methods, however, require the user to provide a
sketch, which is not always a possibility.

© Springer-Verlag GmbH Germany, part of Springer Nature 2018
M. L. Gavrilova et al. (Eds.): Trans. on Comput. Sci. XXXII, LNCS 10830, pp. 90–105, 2018.
https://doi.org/10.1007/978-3-662-56672-5_7

Motivated by the above mentioned potential applications and the limitation of current face image synthesis technologies, we aim to develop a novel system that can generate an image of a face from a user's imagination or memory through some simple user interactions. In the proposed system, a set of example images are used to train an Optimum-Path Forest (OPF) algorithm to classify the face images based on their relevance to the face in the user's mind. We favour OPF over other classification algorithms because it is fast, simple, multi-class, parameter independent, and not making any assumption about the shapes of the classes [16]. The training process is conducted through a relevance feedback approach. All the user must do under this method is to indicate whether the image of the face shown bears a general resemblance to the face that he or she is imagining, thereby eliminating the need to evaluate individual parts and features separately (as is the case with the montage approach) or visualise or verbalise specific characteristics (as is the case with caricatures).

The remainder of the paper is arranged as follows. Section 2 reviews the related works. Section 3 describes the algorithm in detail. In Sect. 4, the experimental results are demonstrated and discussed.

2   Related Works

Although face recognition is one of the most active research fields in computer vision, to the best of the authors' knowledge, there are few studies that have been conducted on the synthesis of face images. With the montage approach to face image synthesis [2], the user looks through a database of various face components (e.g., eyebrows, eyes, noses, mouths, etc.) for the ones that most closely match the image in his or her imagination or memory. The selected features are then synthesised into a face image. The process requires the user to search for each part separately and make isolated judgments on resemblance; the user looks only at the eyes when looking for the eyes that approximate those of the face in his or her mind. Again, this is another challenging task. Finding the ideal combination of parts can take a considerable amount of time, as well. E-FIT [1], a montage synthesis system that facilitates the creation of 3-D, computer generated faces, narrows down the search range by age and sex and lets the user make post-synthesis tweaks to facial feature sizes and positions to make the final face models more accurate. However, the effectiveness of E-FIT in generating a face model also depends on the user's past experience with modelling and sensitivity to various face features.

Wu and Dai [3] present method for synthesising face images according to sketches. By querying a face image database using different parts of a face sketch, the corresponding face parts with the highest degrees of resemblance are patched together to form a final image. The users can adjust the size, shape and colour of face parts to make the resulting face accurate. However, these methods require the user to draw a sketch- a talent that not everyone has.

Kurt et al. [4] proposed a semiautomatic method that uses a genetic algorithm to update feature parameters to synthesize a face image. Since their technique uses the AAM (Active Appearance Model) [4] for modelling and synthesizing face images, facial features in the areas with no high frequency information cannot be captured.

The face hallucination technique [5, 6] uses information from a face image database to synthesise high-resolution images from low-resolution images. One potential application of this method is to synthesize high-resolution images from the grainy, low-resolution images captured by surveillance cameras. The image database is used to compute probable high-resolution features from the low-resolution images. Most recently, deep learning based techniques have been combined with face hallucination [7], making it possible to generate high-resolution images from images with very low-resolution and unconstrained pose.

However, prior methods based on feature mapping and deep learning could not be employed to estimate facial features in the absence of a reference image. For example, sketch based method heavily relies on a sketch face image; face hallucination method requires a low-resolution image as the input. Our method can generate face images that are satisfactory to the user demands without needing to seek clues from a reference image.

Our system uses an active learning scheme to narrow the gap between low-level image features and high-level semantic understanding. Recently, active learning algorithms combining conventional machine learning techniques with relevance feedback have been attracted large attentions. For example, in Content-Based Image Retrieval (CBIR) systems, Support Vector Machine (SVM) based active learning schemes are used for efficient image data clustering. Liu *et al.* [8] presented an SVM-based relevance feedback technique for image retrieval on small database. Wang *et al.* [9] combined a few one-class SVM classifiers to boost the retrieval performance. Wang *et al.* [10] introduced a Neural Network (NN)-based method for CBIR and evaluated their algorithm on a database of 2,000 images. However, with the growing sample data, SVM [16] and NN algorithms become less efficient than Random Forest (RF) and Optimum-Path Forest methods (OPF) [18] in handling multi-class classification. Fu and Qiu [11] developed an RF-based image retrieval framework and examined their system in image-based and keyword-based image retrieval scenarios. The RF was generated based on semantic similarity measure. Although RF runs quite efficient, if the sample distribution is uneven, the classification result is unreliable. Based on these observations, we employ an OPF-based relevance feedback technique.

3 Proposed Method

As depicted in Fig. 1, the proposed system includes three major components: extracting primary features, training an OPF classifier based on relevance feedback, and synthesising face images that do not already exist in the database.

In our study, we used 1,000 sample images in the training database. These images were converted to a feature space for training an OPF algorithm to classify whether a face image resembles the face in the users' minds based on their relevance feedback. The ultimate purpose of our method is not to classify those sample face images or to retrieve a particular face from these sample face images but to synthesise a new image resembling the face in the user's mind. The trained OPF classifier defines the positions in the feature space that correspond to the desired face images.

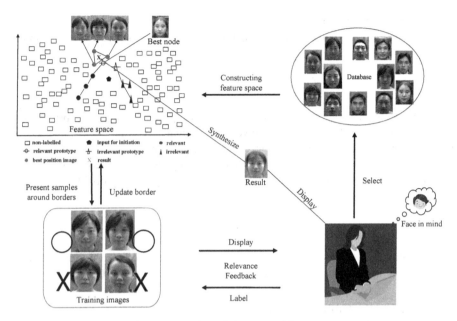

Fig. 1. Overview of the proposed system

To train the OPF classifier, the system defines an initial classification boundary by letting the users evaluate an initial dataset consisting of face images of different sexes and ages. Then, the system shows the user multiple unevaluated images (i.e. cases that have not been judged by the user to resemble or not resemble the picture in his or her mind) that lie near the classification boundary and has the user label them according to whether they resemble or do not resemble the face in his or her mind. Based on these labels, the system updates the classification boundary.

Then, the system interpolates K cases in the positions farthest from the classification boundary on the positive side and produces the final synthesis. If the results satisfy the user, the search process is complete; otherwise, the user repeats the labelling process on unlabelled cases near the classification boundary.

3.1 Constructing the Feature Space

Various feature representations have been studied in the context of face recognition in the past few decades. Recent research results have demonstrated that deep learning can be used to learn the face representation, which is effective for both face identification and verification [12, 13].

However, since our purpose was to synthesise a target face image, we needed a feature representation that could not only discriminate faces but could also be used to generate a face image. The feature vector space needed to be compact enough to allow for the interactive relevance feedback process. For this purpose, we used the pixel-level image feature used in the face hallucination method [5].

The basic idea is to separate a face image I into a global image I_g, which expresses the overall features of the image, and a local image I_l, which expresses the detailed face features.

$$I = I_g + I_l. \tag{1}$$

While the local image adds the details of the face, global images comprise information required for distinguishing between individuals. A feature vector space of global images can be constructed by applying principal component analysis to the face images in the database and finding the principal components with large eigenvalues. Formula (2) expresses a global image I in terms of the basis B of a global feature space, a coordinate value X and an average face image μ:

$$I = BX + \mu. \tag{2}$$

Our study uses the global feature space as the search space for locating the coordinates of the image that best matches the corresponding face in mind.

3.2 Training the Optimum-Path Forest Classifier Based on Relevance Feedback

Relevance feedback, a process that shows synthesis results to the users and updates classifiers based on user feedback, is often used in image retrieval with specific themes, such as oceans, cats or sunsets. Several researchers have proposed methods that employ various classifier types and reuse past classification results to obtain good results based on relatively minimal amounts of feedback [14–16].

Our study used the OPF [16–18] for classification. The OPF works by modelling the classification as a graph partition in a given feature space. It starts as a complete graph whose nodes represent the feature vectors of all images in the database. All pairs of nodes are linked by arcs that are weighted by the distances between the feature vectors of the corresponding nodes (referred to as costs hereafter). Given a set of training nodes, a minimum spanning tree can be generated from the complete graph. Then, the adjacent training nodes are marked as prototypes if they belong to different classes. We used two classes: relevant and irrelevant. The partition of the graph is carried out by the competition process among the prototypes, which offer optimum paths to the remaining nodes of the graph. The optimum paths from the prototypes to the other samples are computed by the image foresting transform algorithm, which is essentially Dijkstra's algorithm modified for multiple sources and with more general path-value functions. Finally, all of the non-prototypes are directly or indirectly connected with the prototype that has the minimum cost. With the prototypes as the roots and the non-prototypes as the intermediate and terminal nodes, the optimum trees are built, which constitutes the OPF. OPF performs well with samples represented in a complex and high-dimension feature space. Because of this, OPF is very important in systems that are based on the relevance feedback approach and generate results in a dialogic fashion.

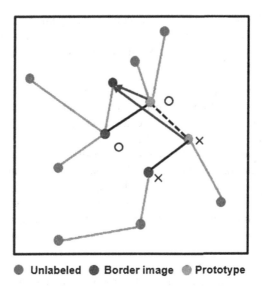

● Unlabeled   ● Border image   ● Prototype

Fig. 2. Overview of the Optimum-Path Forest algorithm (Color figure online)

Figure 2 shows an example of a classification with OPF. A minimum spanning tree is first constructed from all the samples. Then, the user labels some selected samples as positive (○) or negative (×). We thus focus on the paths that bridge positive and negative samples. The nodes bridged by the paths are called prototypes, which are represented as green dots. All other unlabelled nodes whose parent is a positive prototype are labelled as positive, and the ones whose parent is a negative prototype are labelled as negative. The nodes next to the prototypes are called border nodes as indicated by the red dots. The node located the farthest from the negative prototype and closest to the positive prototype (depicted by the purple node in the figure) is selected as the best positive sample.

As depicted in Fig. 1, the OPF is trained based on the users' relevance feedbacks in the following four steps:

1. The system presents the user with five male face images and five female face images of different ages and waits for the user to select one he or she thinks to be closest to the face in his or her mind. Since none of those 10 images is likely to resemble the target face, the user will select the image that is the most similar to what they are imagining according to sex and age, which acts as the initial classification boundary.

2. The four images closest to the user's selected face image in the feature spaces are returned to the user. The user evaluates and labels the images as positive (○) or negative (×), which serve as the prototypes for the OPF classifier. This evaluation phase ends if the users are satisfied with at least one of the four face images.

3. An OPF classifier is built based on this set as illustrated in Fig. 2. Then, the OPF classifier divides the unlabelled images of the database into two classes: relevant and irrelevant.

4. Four border nodes are selected, and the corresponding images are presented to the users. The user evaluates and labels the images as positive (O) or negative (×), and the new marked training images constitute and replace the former training samples to build a new OPF classifier.

At every iteration before step 4, the best positive nodes located the farthest to negative prototype and the closest to positive prototype are selected and interpolated to create the resulting face image being presented to the user. If the user is satisfied, the whole relevance feedback procedure ends.

When selecting the border nodes and the best positive nodes, we compare the costs of paths from all non-training nodes to all relevant and irrelevant prototypes. The training samples are the four images which belong to the relevant class and have the smallest ratio between the cost to the relevant prototypes and the cost to the irrelevant prototypes. The best positive nodes are those that belong to the relevant class and with the largest ratio between the cost to the relevant prototypes and the costs to the irrelevant prototypes.

In our implementation, the cost of the arc connecting two adjacent nodes of the OPF feature space is calculated with the L2 norm. Assuming there are k number of relevant prototypes and m number of irrelevant ones represented as $p_i(i = 1, 2, \ldots k)$ and $q_j(j = 1, 2, \ldots m)$ respectively, we consider $k \times m$ pairs of (p_i, q_j) in computing the ratio of the path costs to the relevant and irrelevant prototypes. Let $CR_{U \to p_i}$ represent the cost of the path from the non-training sample U to the relevant prototype p_i, and let $CI_{U \to q_j}$ represent the cost of the path from U to the irrelevant prototype q_j. $Relevance_{U \to (p_i, q_j)}$ which represents the ratio of $CR_{U \to p_i}$ to $CI_{U \to q_j}$, is computed as Formula (3):

$$Relevance_{U \to (p_i, q_j)} = \left(\frac{CR_{Ur} \to p_i}{CI_{Ur} \to q_j} \right). \tag{3}$$

In the traditional relevance feedback-based image retrieval, the final result is the positive case in the position farthest from the classification boundary. To establish the classification boundary correctly, the image shown to the user for feedback must lie near the classification boundary. OPF based retrieval thus requires an initial classification boundary that sits relatively close to the positive case. Our study satisfied this requirement by gathering age and sex input information at the beginning of the process.

3.3   Synthesising Virtual Face Images Using Interpolation

The traditional relevance feedback approach is designed for searching actual images in a given database, making it impossible to synthesise non-existent face images. By synthesising images, however, it is possible to obtain the desired outcomes with a limited number of samples. Our study thus proposes a process of synthesizing face images that do not exist in the database by interpolating multiple positive images in positions far away from the classification boundary. In principle, any point near the best positive node (i.e. the node that belongs to the relevant class and with the largest ratio between the cost to the relevant prototypes and the costs to the irrelevant prototypes) should be a desired face image.

As a practical solution, we select the top k ($k = 3$ in the current implementation) best positive nodes as shown in Fig. 1, and calculate the result according to the following Formula (4):

$$x = \sum_{i}^{k} w(x_i)x_i / \sum_{i}^{k} w(x_i). \tag{4}$$

Here, x and x_i ($i = 0, 1, 2$) are the feature vectors of the resulting face images and the 3 best positive images, respectively. The weight assigned to x_i is $w(x_i)$, which is based on the distance given by the classifier. In the current implementation, $w(x_i)$ is assigned the average weight, which means all 3 images have equal weight.

3.4 Registration by Eyes and Mouth

The sample images in the training database need to be aligned in order to create face images without blurring. In cases where the same images aligned only by one single registration point when synthesising new face images by interpolating several face images, the system was prone to blurring portions of the face away from the registration point due to the inherent individual variations among these different faces. Figure 4(a) and (b) show the results generated with the images were aligned by eye position and mouth position only, respectively. We can see that areas far from the registration areas are severely blurred.

To solve this problem, we built two image databases from the same source database: one composed of face images aligned by the eyes and the other composed of face images aligned by the mouth. In order to synthesise a clear face image, a group of images from the eye-aligned database and the corresponding images from the mouth-aligned database are used. More specifically, three procedures are carried out: first, a candidate image in the eye-aligned face feature space is synthesised; then, another face image in the mouth-aligned space is synthesised; by blending the two images, a clear composited face image is produced.

As the system makes it possible to obtain the same face from both databases, we only need to perform the relevance feedback process with one of the two databases to build the OPF for both databases. Figure 3 illustrates the integration between the feature spaces of the two databases. When selecting the three highest-ranking coordinates in the feature space defined by the images aligned by eyes, for example, the one-to-one correspondence between the two spaces means that we can obtain the corresponding three highest-ranking coordinates in the other feature space built from the examples aligned by the mouth. As the arrows in Fig. 3 show, the system thus enables coordinate matching across the two spaces. Thus, we can synthesise two face images by interpolating the three highest-ranking coordinates in the two spaces, respectively.

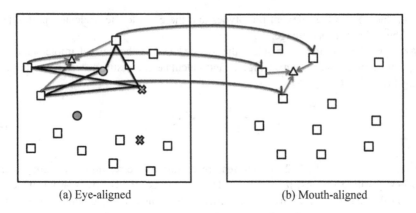

| (a) Eye-aligned | (b) Mouth-aligned |

Fig. 3. Image correspondence between eye-aligned space and mouth-aligned space. In the eye-aligned feature space shown in (a), the yellow ○ and × represent user-labelled images, and the blue ○ and × represent the positive and negative prototypes. The □'s connected to the prototypes by black lines are the three best positive images. The △ represents the generated virtual image interpolated using the three best positive images. The correspondence between the best positive images in the eye-aligned and mouth-aligned spaces are illustrated with red lines. The interpolated virtual image in the mouth-aligned space is shown with a △. (Color figure online)

To fuse the two face images computed from the separately aligned spaces (i.e. the images represented by △ in Fig. 3[a] and [b]) and form a new image with clear face components, α blending is used, as given by Formula (5):

$$I = \alpha I_e + (1 - \alpha)I_m. \tag{5}$$

I_e and I_m are the images from the eye-aligned and mouth-aligned spaces, respectively, and α is the blending weight. We set the value of α to 1 in the area above the eyes, set the value of α to 0 in the area below the mouth, and changed the α value in the area between the eyes and the mouth in linear interpolation. The blended image is further filtered with a bilateral filter to decrease the degree of edge blur.

Figures 4(a), (b) and (c) show the resulting images synthesised in eye-aligned space, mouth-aligned space and by α blending the former two images, respectively.

| (a) Image generated in eye-aligned space | (b) Image generated in mouth-aligned space | (c) Image generated via α blending |

Fig. 4. Comparison between the single point registered result and the result obtained by α blending.

We can see in Fig. 4(a) and (b) that areas far from the registration areas are severely blurred, while in Fig. 4(c), such flaws are alleviated.

4 Experiment and Discussion

4.1 Database

For our sample image set, we used 1,000 images of Asian faces from the CAS-PEAL database [19] and the Cartoon Face database [20]. We made all the images monochrome, and set the resolution to 96 × 128. The database comprised only frontal face images, but the positions and sizes of the faces differed. We resized and cropped the images. Then we created two databases that were aligned by eye positions and mouth positions, respectively. Our study was concerned only with general face features, so we used a low resolution of 96 × 128 for all the images. We set the images to monochrome to prevent colours not found in the original cases from appearing when the system interpolate multiple colour images.

Each dimension of the feature space corresponds to a pixel of the face images. Therefore, the feature vector has 12,288 (96 × 128) dimensions. Based on a primary component analysis, we used the 80 dimensions with the highest eigenvalues as our global face feature space, which provided a cumulative contribution ratio above 80%.

4.2 Experiments

To validate the effectiveness of the proposed method, we had 12 subjects (all university students in their 20s, 11 of whom were male and 1 of whom was female) attend our experiments. During the experiments, we asked the subjects to ignore hairstyles when creating and evaluating the face images because the significant differences in hairstyles among the images in the database led to blurred hair in all the generated images.

We conducted the following three experiments to determine whether the subjects could create satisfactory face images using the system and how long (in terms of time and iteration count) this process would take.

Creating Imagined Face Images. In this experiment, we had each subject imagine a face and let them use the system to create a similar image. Figure 5 shows the created images based on the subjects' imagined faces. In Sect. 4.3, we will evaluate how these created face images resembled the imagined faces.

Creating Face Images Based on Briefly Presented Reference Images. In this experiment, we presented a reference face image that did not exist in the database to each subject for 3–4s and asked the subject to create a face image resembling the reference image to validate whether the system enabled the user to synthesize an image from his or her memory. Such a situation is similar to the case where an eyewitness has seen a criminal's face for a very short time and tries to reconstruct the face image based on his or her rough impression and memory. Figure 6 shows the face images that the

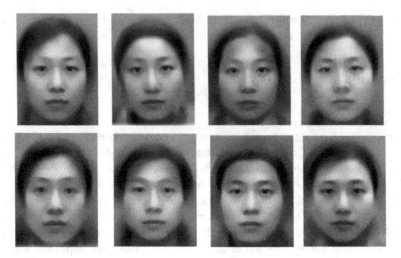

Fig. 5. Images created based on the subjects' imagined faces

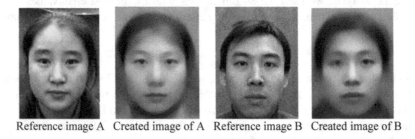

Reference image A   Created image of A   Reference image B   Created image of B

Fig. 6. Reference images shown for 3–4s and the corresponding created images

subjects saw for 3–4s and the corresponding generated face images. As it can be seen from the figures, the resulting images capture some major features of the reference faces, such as the overall shape of faces and the relatively small sizes of the eyes.

Creating Face Images Based on the Reference Images Presented During the Entire Process. For a more objective validation, we conducted a third experiment that presented the subjects with a reference image for the entire duration of the process until they reached a result they found satisfactory. Figure 7 shows two examples of the results. The resulting images maintain a basic consistency with their respective target images.

Figure 8 illustrates how the resulting images actually changed over the process. The target image and the resulting image were noticeably different at first. As the subject went through iterations of the process, the face in the resulting image gradually came to more closely resemble the reference one.

Reference image A   Created image of A   Reference image B   Created image of B

Fig. 7. Reference images shown during the entire experiment and the corresponding created images

Reference image   1st iteration   2nd iteration   3rd iteration   14th iteration

Fig. 8. Changes of the synthesised result over the process

4.3   Evaluation

Evaluation Based on Subjective Scoring. In the three experiments mentioned above, we also asked the subjects to score the results on a five-point scale (1: No resemblance; 2: Very weak resemblance; 3: Neither weak nor strong resemblance; 4: Somewhat strong resemblance; 5: Strong resemblance).

Figure 9 shows the average scores, in which the scores of three experiments are very similar. The average score for all three experiments came to 3.833. Many of the subjects declared that they were satisfied once the created images began to bear a somewhat resemblance to the target faces. Figure 10 shows the times (in seconds) that it took the subjects to arrive at satisfactory results.

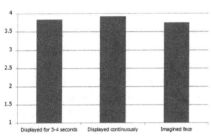
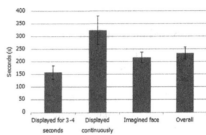

Fig. 9. Average final scores   **Fig. 10.** Average time to final results (in seconds)

Figure 11 shows the number of iterations that it took the subjects to arrive at satisfactory results. Figure 12, meanwhile, illustrates the changes in scores for three subjects during the relevance feedback process. Each line represents a single iteration of the process by an individual subject. On average, it took 6.5 iterations for the subjects to arrive at the final results.

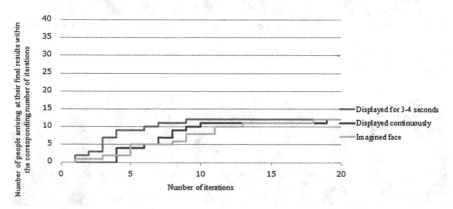

Fig. 11. Iteration numbers of each experiment. The vertical axis of the graph represents the number of subjects who reached their final results with the number of iterations shown on the horizontal axis.

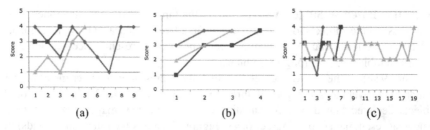

Fig. 12. Changes in scores during the relevance feedback process: (a) Creating an imagined face image, (b) Creating a face image based on briefly (3–4s) presented reference images, and (c) Creating a face image based on the reference image presented during the entire process.

Evaluation Based on Matching Test. To evaluate the effectiveness of our method, we conducted a matching test by letting a group of participants creating face images using the system from reference images, and then having another group of participants match the generated images with their reference images. In this test, 10 peoples of different age (5 in 20s, 1 in 30s, 3 in 40s and 1 in 50s) and gender (6 male and 4 female) were asked to synthesize face image, while another 13 peoples of different age (9 in 20s, 4 in 40s and 1 in 50s) and gender (10 male and 4 female) were asked to attend the matching test relating the synthesize image to the right reference image. We performed the test as the following 2 steps.

Face image generating step: we randomly choose 20 face images (12 female and 8 male) from the test image database as reference images. Each of the 10 subjects participated the face image generation was given 2 different reference images randomly selected from these 20 images and be asked to synthesize 1 face based on each reference image. Therefore, we obtained 20 synthesized face images generated from the 20 difference reference images.

Image matching step: For each of the 13 subjects participated the image matching test, we randomly divided the 20 pairs of synthesized image and references image into 10 groups. Each group contains 2 pairs of synthesized image and references image of the same gender. Thus, we have 6 female pairs and 4 male pairs. Then, the 10 groups were shown to the subject one by one, and for each group the subject was asked to match between the generated image and the reference image. Since each of the 13 subjects performed the matching task for 10 groups, the total number of trial was 130. Out of which, 100 trials gave a correct matching result. A binominal test showed that the generated images were correctly matched to their corresponding reference image at a significance level above 99%. The result demonstrates that our system can generate images resembling the reference images.

Evaluation: In Fig. 13, we gave a couple of successfully matching image groups (100% match), the upper row, and worst matching groups in our experiments, the lower row. For image C, 6 in 13 participants correctly matched the reference image and created image, while for image D, 7 in 13 participants correctly matched the reference image and created image. The reason participants mismatched the images may be complex; we found majority of them thought the look in the eyes or facial expression are different.

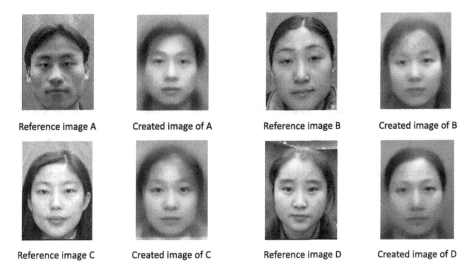

| Reference image A | Created image of A | Reference image B | Created image of B |

| Reference image C | Created image of C | Reference image D | Created image of D |

Fig. 13. The examples used for matching test.

4.4 Discussions

The results of the experiment reveal several findings. When we displayed the reference images for 3–4s and then had the subjects create their images without being able to see the original references, the subjects took fewer iterations and less time to arrive at their results than they did when the reference image was presented throughout the whole process. This is likely because the images were only visible to the subjects for a matter of seconds, which made it hard for the subjects to establish a clear, accurate mental picture of the target face for comparison. Thus, the system-generated images probably created a slight recognition bias in the subjects' minds, leading them to converge on their final results relatively quickly. The subjects' evaluations of the resulting images showed several interesting trends, as well. In many cases, the evaluation scores remained relatively constant for several iterations before eventually increasing. This is because the experiment used the three highest-ranking results. Even if we were to have shuffled the rankings of the three images, their relative mutual similarity and central position would have resulted in the same generated face and produced the same score.

Some users reported that sometimes they were satisfied with most parts of the generated face after a few iterations, but unsatisfied with one particular part. The users then continued the iteration process in anticipation of getting a better result for that particular part. But unfortunately, they obtained a globally worse image with other satisfying parts became less satisfied. Although allowing the users to evaluate and control the face as a whole is an advantage of our method over the component-based approaches like montage system, it is desirable to improve our system by allowing the users to locally adjust individual parts.

Another drawback of current implementation lies in our feature representation. We employed a global feature space based on PCA which fail to capture the personal detail well, causing the generated face quite similar to the average face. As a major future work, we will explore better feature representation including using Convolutional Neural Network.

5   Conclusion and Future Work

In this paper, we proposed a method for the semiautomatic synthesis of a face image from a user's imagination. By training an OPF based on the user's feedback, our system successfully creates synthesised images that resembled the face images that users had in mind. One potential avenue for future work related to this paper is to explore other feature representations, such as the Convolutional Neural Network.

Acknowledgement. This work was supported by JSPS KAKENHI (Grant No. 17H00737) and the Public Projects of Zhejiang Natural Science Foundation Province, China (Grant No. LGF18F020015).

References

1. E-FIT. http://www.visionmetric.com/
2. Wang, X., Tang, X.: Face photo-sketch synthesis and recognition. IEEE Trans. Pattern Anal. Mach. Intell. **31**(11), 1955–1967 (2009)
3. Wu, D., Dai, Q.: Sketch realizing: lifelike portrait synthesis from sketch. In: Computer Graphics International Conference, pp. 13–20 (2009)
4. Cootes, T., Edwards, G., Taylor, C.: Active appearance models. IEEE Trans. Pattern Anal. Mach. Intell. **23**(6), 681–685 (2001)
5. Liu, C., Shum, H., Freeman, W.: Face hallucination: theory and practice. Int. J. Comput. Vision **75**(1), 115–134 (2007)
6. Gao, X., Yang, J., Lai, Z., Huang, P., Jiang, J., Gao, H., Yue, D.: Nuclear norm regularized coding with local position-patch and nonlocal similarity for face hallucination. Digit. Signal Proc. **64**, 107–120 (2017)
7. Zhu, S., Liu, S., Loy, C., Tang, X.: Deep cascaded bi-network for face hallucination. In: Computer Vision and Pattern Recognition, pp. 614–630 (2016)
8. Liu, R., Wang, Y., Baba, T., Masumoto, D., Nagata, S.: SVM-based active feedback in image retrieval using clustering and unlabeled data. Pattern Recogn. **41**(8), 2645–2655 (2008)
9. Xiang, Y., Yang, H., Li, Y., Chen, J.: A new SVM-based active feedback scheme for image retrieval. Eng. Appl. Artif. Intell. **37**, 43–53 (2015)
10. Wang, B., Zhang, X., Li, N.: Relevance feedback technique for content-based image retrieval using neural network learning. In: International Conference on Machine Learning and Cybernetics (2006)
11. Fu, H., Qiu, G.: Fast semantic image retrieval based on random forest. In: International Conference on Multimedia, pp. 909–912 (2012)
12. Sun, Y., Chen, Y., Wang, X., Tang, X.: Deep learning face representation by joint identification-verification. In: Advances in Neural Information Processing Systems, pp. 1988–1996 (2014)
13. Sun, Y., Wang, X., Tang, X.: Deep learning face representation from predicting 10,000 classes. In: Computer Vision and Pattern Recognition, pp. 1891–1898 (2014)
14. Ruthven, I., Lalmas, M.: A survey on the use of relevance feedback for information access systems. Knowl. Eng. Rev. **18**(2), 95–145 (2003)
15. Li, H., Toyoura, M., Shimizu, K., Yang, W., Mao, X.: Retrieval of clothing images based on relevance feedback with focus on collar designs. Vis. Comput. **32**(10), 1351–1363 (2016)
16. Silva, A., Falcao, A., Magalhaes, L.: Active learning paradigms for CRIR systems based on optimum-path forest classification. J. WSCG **18**(1–3), 73–80 (2010)
17. Papa, J., Falca, A.: Optimum-path forest: a novel and powerful framework for supervised graph-based pattern recognition techniques, pp. 41–48. Institute of Computing University of Campinas (2010)
18. Papa, J., Falcao, A., Suzuki, C.: Supervised pattern classification based on optimum-path forest. Imaging Syst. Technol. **19**(2), 120–131 (2009)
19. Li, H., Liu, G., Ngan, K.: Guided face cartoon synthesis. IEEE Trans. Multimedia **13**(6), 1230–1239 (2001)
20. Gao, W., Gao, B., Shan, S., Chen, X., Zhou, D., Zhang, X., Zhao, D.: The CAS-PEAL large-scale Chinese face database and baseline evaluations. IEEE Trans. Syst. Man Cybern. Syst. **38**(1), 149–161 (2008)

NeuroFeedback Training for Enhancement of the Focused Attention Related to Athletic Performance in Elite Rifle Shooters

Yisi Liu[1]([✉]), Salem Chandrasekaran Harihara Subramaniam[1],
Olga Sourina[1], Eesha Shah[2], Joshua Chua[2], and Kirill Ivanov[2]

[1] Fraunhofer Singapore, Singapore, Singapore
{liuys, scharihara, eosourina}@ntu.edu.sg
[2] Singapore Sports Institute, Singapore, Singapore
{Eesha_SHAH, Joshua_CHUA}@sport.gov.sg,
kyrill_iv@mail.ru

Abstract. NeuroFeedback Training (NFT) is a type of biofeedback training using Electroencephalogram (EEG) that allows the subjects to do self-regulation during the training according to their real-time brain activities. The purpose of this study is to optimize focused attention in expert rifle shooters with the use of NFT tools and to enhance shooting performance. We designed and implemented an experiment, conducted NFT sessions, and confirmed that NFT can boost performance of the shooters. The efficiency of the NFT was examined by comparing the shooters' performance, their results of standardized tests of general cognitive abilities on the Vienna Test System (VTS), and the brain patterns in before and after NFT sessions. According to the results, we confirmed that NFT can be used to boost the shooters' performance. EEG data were recorded during the shooting tasks. We extracted different types of EEG-based indexes and identified the emotion and mental workload levels of the shooters right before they pulled the trigger. These indexes and emotion/workload levels were then correlated with the shooting scores to understand what are the optimal brain states for "good" shots. According to the results, we confirmed that (1) mental workload level is negatively correlated with the shooting performance; (2) the correlations analyses results between EEG-based power features and shooting performance are consistent with the literature review results; (3) the difference of brain states in the before and after NFT shooting session could be because of NFT.

Keywords: NeuroFeedback · Performance of athletes
Individual frequency range · EEG · Rifle shooters · Mental workload
Emotions

1 Introduction

Nowadays, athletes are facing more and more challenges and a higher competition. To look for ways how to enhance performance following the rules in sport, various research is done. Sports nutrition is one of the research focuses to improve athletes'

© Springer-Verlag GmbH Germany, part of Springer Nature 2018
M. L. Gavrilova et al. (Eds.): Trans. on Comput. Sci. XXXII, LNCS 10830, pp. 106–119, 2018.
https://doi.org/10.1007/978-3-662-56672-5_8

performance. For example, the dietary intakes and food consumed were studied in [1]; hydration strategies were emphasized in [2]. Besides that, a lot of work has been done on the strategy for physical preparation. For example, the training intensity was investigated in [3]; the influence of different high-intensity interval training was studied in [4]; the effect of core stability and strength was discussed in [5]. In addition to the physical preparation, mental preparation plays a decisive role in optimizing the performance. Traditional sports psychological training includes meditation [6], goal setting, positive thinking and self-talk, concentration and routines, arousal regulation techniques, and imagery [7], etc. Novel training such as biosignal-based training is being introduced recently. In this paper, we study the Electroencephalogram (EEG)-based NeuroFeedback Training (NFT) to improve shooters' performance. Compared with other strategies, EEG signals can reflect the inner and true feelings of the user, and NFT allows them to do self-regulation without the participation of psychologists.

In our previous work [8], a preliminary experiment with 5 elite shooters participating in up to 7 NFT sessions was described. The efficiency of NFT was analyzed by the shooting performance and results of DAUF test from Vienna Test System (VTS) to assess cognitive abilities such as sustained attention of the shooters before and after training. The results showed that the majority of the shooters gained improvement in the scores after up to 7 NFT sessions. In this paper, we extended the work described in [8] with analyses of physiological indexes calculated from EEG. Standardized alpha, beta, theta/beta ratio, SMR, beta1, and beta2 were extracted from EEG and analyzed to study correlation between the EEG-based indexes and the shooters' performance results before and after NFT. The definitions of the EEG rhythms are given in Sect. 2.1. Brain states such as emotions and workload levels were identified and the correlations with the shooters' performance results before and after NFT were analyzed. Based on the results, it is revealed that the NFT changed the correlations, in other words, the brain states could be adjusted by NFT.

To recognize emotions and workload levels, the algorithms proposed in our previous work [9, 10] were applied. Fractal dimension and statistical features were extracted from the raw EEG data and used to train the Support Vector Machine (SVM) classifier. The saved SVM model then was used to identify the brain states during shooting before and after NFT.

The paper is organized as follows. Section 2 reviews the EEG rhythms, NFT protocols for performance optimization, and Vienna test. Section 3 introduces the proposed experiment design and NFT settings. Section 4 presents effect of NFT and Sect. 5 concludes the paper.

2   Related Work

2.1   EEG Rhythms

EEG rhythms can be categorized to five bands according to the frequency ranges. The rhythm from 0.5–4 Hz is defined as delta wave. It is associated with deep sleep however can still be presented while the subject is awake [11]. Theta band ranges from 4–8 Hz, which is related to drowsy state. Recent research also finds that training-down theta power can help to improve the verbal IQ, executive functions and attention for seniors [12] and be used as the training protocol to deal with mental disorder such as Attention Deficit Hyperactivity Disorder (ADHD) [13, 14]. The alpha wave, which ranges from 8 to 12 Hz, is associated with relaxation, meditation and a lack of concentration and attention to any specific tasks or objects. Beta wave, of which the frequency range is from 12 to 30 Hz, is always apparent when a subject is actively thinking about something or focusing on an object or task [11]. Unlike theta wave, beta power is always trained-up in ADHD treatment [13, 14] and it also shows that training up the beta power can help to reduce the reaction time in the attention test for healthy subjects [15]. The last group of brain wave, 30 Hz and above, is called gamma wave. This wave is much more rarely observed and tends to indicate the presence of a brain disease.

2.2   NeuroFeedback Training for Performance Optimization

In recent years, researchers have started to focus on performance optimization of shooters using NFT [16, 17]. In [16], the effect of NFT was investigated on expert rifle shooters and two NFT protocols were used in this study. One involved increasing the sensorimotor rhythm (SMR, 13–15 Hz) while inhibiting high-beta (20–30 Hz) whereas the other involved training crossover between alpha (8–12 Hz) and theta (4–8 Hz) with high-beta suppression. The results revealed that the marksmen who underwent NFT showed significant improvements in performance after fifteen sessions of NFT comparing with control group [16]. Besides rifle shooters, study about the impact of NFT on air-pistol shooters was done in [18–22]. In [18], Event Related Desynchronization/ Synchronization (ERD/ERS) in lower alpha (8–10 Hz), higher alpha (10–12 Hz), beta (16–24 Hz) and theta (4–8 Hz) frequency band was analyzed to identify the neural markers associated with optimal and sub-optimal performance in air-pistol shooters. The results of the study concluded that optimal and sub-optimal performance was associated with a different cortical pattern and ideal performance occurred with an increase in the lower alpha band which was associated with relaxation states. Based on this finding, it was suggested that a NFT protocol could be increasing lower alpha as it led to improvement in the performance. In [19], the effect of cortico-cortical communication on disabled and non-disabled elite air-pistol shooters was investigated. The results revealed that disabled shooters with spinal cord injury had higher coherence in all brain regions of higher alpha (11–13 Hz), and only frontal and central regions of beta (14–35 Hz), and gamma (36–44 Hz) frequency bands compared with non-disabled shooters. These results were used to reduce activation in task-irrelevant cortical areas and hence suggested that application of appropriate NFT can improve the performance of disabled shooters. Work [20] used the NFT protocol of increasing left temporal alpha power and the results showed that after NFT, both left temporal alpha power and shooting scores were improved. In [21], it showed that by increasing beta 1 and SMR amplitude in pistol shooters, they were able to reduce irrelevant muscles activities during shooting, which in result, led to better psychomotor function and cognitive control. Following the protocol in [21], [22] showed that by enhancing beta 1 and SMR amplitude while inhibiting theta band, the autotelic engagement of attention of athletes was improved.

In other areas of sports, NFT is also used to optimize the performance of athletes. For example, studies have been carried out with individuals in the fields of archery and golf [23–25]. The training protocol involved the self-regulation of SMR frequency which corresponds to deceleration of heart rate and improvement in archery performance [23]. In [24], a research was conducted with a group of golfers. The correlation between sensorimotor alpha and beta rhythm with upright balance and arm movement control were investigated. As successful golf putts were characterized by high frequency alpha, [24] concluded that a NFT protocol to increase the alpha band frequency in golfers will enhance their performance. The effect of NFT for golfers was studied in [25]. The golfers were trained to reduce their frontal high-alpha power before striking. The results showed that golfers were able to give robust performance even under high pressure conditions which can be accredited to the NFT.

Another commonly used protocol for NFT to achieve positive effects on performance in sports, posture rehabilitation, and treatment of Attention Deficit Hyperactivity Disorder (ADHD) is to train the ratio of beta to theta power [26–29]. [26] has researched on the use of beta/theta ratio to study physical balance and posture improvement. It is claimed that regulating corresponding brain activity has improved the physical balance in individuals with balance problems. The meta-analysis investigating the theta/beta ratio in ADHD groups showed that the healthier control groups have lesser theta/beta ratio whereas the ADHD groups showed higher ratio values in [27]. The experiment also warranted the use of theta/beta ratio as both a prognostic measure and a reliable diagnostic measure of ADHD. An experiment to measure the attention level of individuals by using machine learning approach on the EEG data has shown that self-regulation of theta/beta ratio was important to overcome ADHD symptoms and improve attention levels [28]. In [29], the effect of NFT on attention deficit children was studied and the training protocol aimed at suppression of theta band (4–8 Hz) and improvement of beta band (13–20 Hz). The results showed that children who had attended NFT gained behavioral improvements.

Besides the use of standard frequency range of EEG, there are works studying individual frequency based NFT. For example, [30] showed that individual frequency range based NFT was more efficient compared to standard range. In our previous work [31], we compared the EEG-based NFT using individual upper alpha power and individual beta/theta ratio. The results showed that using ratio-based training was less affected by artifacts. We also further proofed the usage of ratio-based training in enhancing the individual alpha peak and alpha bandwidth in [17]. Thus in this paper, we employed the individual beta/theta based NFT, which is further explained in Sect. 3.

2.3   Vienna Test – DAUF for Sustained Attention

The Vienna Test System provides a series of psychological tests which can be used to measure the cognitive ability of the testees [32]. For example, it can measure spatial visualization, focused attention, concentration, etc., and be used to assess the suitability for certain jobs, in our research, namely the potential for elite shooters. In this work, we use the DAUF test to assess the ability of sustained attention of the shooters. There are three test forms. As Form 1 and 2 are mainly for clinical usage, we apply Form 3 which is for normal usage in our study. In Form 3, 7 triangles are shown in one row and the testee needs to react when three of them point downwards as illustrated in Fig. 1. Additionally, the changes in row position are irregular. The main variables of DAUF include sum correct which indicate the total number of correct reaction to the desired stimuli, mean time correct which shows the mean reaction time for correct response, sum incorrect which gives the total number of incorrect reaction, and mean time incorrect which shows the mean reaction time for incorrect response.

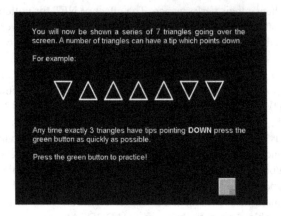

Fig. 1. DAUF test from VTS [32].

3   Methods

In order to assess how NFT can improve performance in shooters we carried out an experiment where NFT was given to the athletes.

3.1   Experiment Design

The experiment design is shown in Table 1. 5 female shooters were involved in the experiment. All shooters are from Singapore national team. Though due to recruiting time limit, only 5 elite shooters managed to attend the experiment, it is a start to investigate the effect of NFT on shooters. These shooters have undergone up to 7 sessions of EEG-based NFT. Before and after NFT the 10 m air rifle shooting sessions were conducted and are used as an index of shooting performance. The EEG data were recorded during the shooting sessions (Fig. 2) and NFT session. Emotiv device [33] with 14 channels were used in the experiment to collect EEG data. All subjects fulfilled an intake questionnaire at the first time when they came to the shooting range.

3.2   NeuroFeedback Protocol

The shooters went through 6 NFT sessions. The NFT protocol was to enhance beta-1/theta ratio (suppress theta/beta-1 ratio).

Table 1. Experiment design.

Phase of study	Duration	Purpose
Familiarization	1 h	Lab-based DAUF test
Pre-training	1 h	Lab-based DAUF test
Pre-training	2 h	(1) EEG-based emotion and workload recognition calibration
		(2) 1 min open/1 min close eyes recording
		(3) Dry Fire – 15 shots
		(4) To record EEG during 40 shots at shooting range as shown in Fig. 2
NFT	30 min × 6 sessions	1 min open/1 min close eyes recording
		10 min lab-based NFT
		1 min open/1 min close eyes recording
Post-training	1 h	Lab-based DAUF test

Fig. 2. Subject wearing EEG device at the shooting range.

To decide the frequency range of beta-1 and theta which is used in the NFT, the individual alpha peak frequency and bandwidth is calculated. As the individual alpha band is suppressed in eyes-open EEG data and dominant in eyes-closed EEG data, we recorded one minute eyes-open and one minute eyes-closed EEG data to obtain the individual alpha band. According to [30, 34], alpha peak frequency is the maximum frequency of the power spectral density in the eye-closed EEG curve and alpha bandwidth is the intersected range of the power spectral density in eyes-open and eyes-closed EEG curves. With the individual alpha band obtained, we can define the individual theta band from 3 Hz to the lower alpha boundary, and the beta-1 band from the upper alpha boundary to 18 Hz.

Among all 14 channels of Emotiv device, P8 from parietal lobe was chosen to be used in the NFT according to our previous work [17]. A shooting game was used in the NFT session (Fig. 3). When the beta-1/theta ratio value is larger than threshold, the color of the robots changes from blue to red and the subject is able to destroy the robots. The subjects need to adjust the brain state from undesired to desired one based

Fig. 3. NFT shooting game.

on the feedback from the NFT game and learn to maintain that state as long as possible during the game. The shooting game was chosen as it is closer to the rifle shooter's expertise.

3.3   NeuroFeedback Procedure

The procedure of the NFT is given in Table 2. The subject needed to fill a question-naire which is about the feeling on that day before the NFT such as is there any headache, any medicine taken before the NFT. Then, the 1 min eyes-closed and eyes-opened EEG was recorded. These recordings were used to calculate the individual alpha peak frequency and individual alpha bandwidth to get the range for the individual beta-1 and theta frequency. Then, the theta/beta-1 ratio during open eyes was calculated from the recorded EEG and used for NFT. The subject needed to complete one 10 min sub-session that includes NFT game playing. After that, the subject needed to record 1 min eye-closed and eyes-open EEG again. Finally, she was asked to fill another two questionnaires which is about sleep diary and feelings after NFT such as tiredness, the strategies used during the game to achieve the desired brain state.

Table 2. Protocol of NFT session.

Steps		Condition	Duration	Electrophysiological records
1	Fill a questionnaire	EO	5 min	–
2	Rest	EC	1 min	Raw EEG (µV, 128 Hz)
		EO	1 min	
3	NFT	EO	10 min	Raw EEG (µV, 128 Hz)
4	Rest	EC	1 min	Raw EEG (µV, 128 Hz)
		EO	1 min	
5	Fill questionnaires	EO	10 min	–

While playing the NFT game, the subjects were first asked to try the strategy they are familiar with in the shooting experience. Other instructions such as fingers heating [35], abdominal breathing [36], Expiration prolongation [37], Position stability [38],

Forehead muscle relaxation [39], Nice imagination [40] were given for the subjects to try to change the colour of the robots from blue to red.

4 Results

4.1 Performance in Shooting Before and After-NFT

To validate the impact of the NFT on the shooters, we compared the total score of two shooting sessions which was carried out before and after NFT respectively as shown in Table 3. Here S1 denotes the shooting session before NFT, and S2 is the shooting session after NFT. Each session is comprised of 40 shots and the total score is tabulated in Table 3. From the table we can conclude that the NFT helped in the shooting performance as Subject 2, 4, and 5 had improvement of the shooting scores. Subject 1 and 3 seemingly had worse score after NFT. So we further examined the distribution of the shooting scores before and after NFT. The 25th, 50th, and 75th percentiles in terms of the shooting score are presented in Table 4. From the distribution, we don't see a significantly drop of the score for Subject 1 and 3. However, we can see Subject 2, 4, 5 have both total score and distribution improved.

Table 3. Total score for before and after NFT.

Subject ID	Session ID	
	S1	S2
	Total score	Total score
1	415.3	414.9
2	414.4	417.3
3	412.7	409.2
4	411.7	412.3
5	410.9	416.4

Table 4. Percentile of the shooting score.

Subject ID	Session ID	Percentile		
		25%	50%	75%
1	S1	10.2	10.4	10.6
	S2	10.2	10.4	10.6
2	S1	10.1	10.4	10.6
	S2	10.2	10.5	10.6
3	S1	10.1	10.4	10.5
	S2	10	10.2	10.6
4	S1	10.1	10.3	10.5
	S2	10.1	10.4	10.6
5	S1	10	10.3	10.5
	S2	10.2	10.4	10.6

Another interesting phenomenon we observed from Table 3 is that subject 5 gained the most significant improvement of total shooting score when before and after NFT results are compared. Considering the shooting score before NFT of Subject 5 is the lowest one, this observation may give us a hint that NFT is more efficient in helping subjects whose ability is relatively lower as there is more space to improve.

Additionally, the coaches of the participated shooters gave thresholds of each shooter, using which we are able to identify how many good shots were in the before and after NFT. The comparison is given in Table 5. Again, except subject 1 and 3, all the other subjects got improved shooting performance after NFT.

Table 5. Number of good shots before and after NFT.

Subject ID	Session ID	
	S1	S2
1	22	21
2	23	25
3	21	13
4	15	15
5	26	32

The paired t-test was applied to the total score and number of good shots of before and after NFT shooting sessions, however, no significant difference was found.

4.2   Performance in DAUF Test Before and After-NFT

The results of before and after NFT DAUF test are presented in Table 6. From this table we can conclude that the performance in DAUF is quite compatible with the total shooting score in Table 3, where Subject 1 and 3 did not achieve improvement after NFT. However, from the result we can see that for Subject 3, there was no difference between "sum correct" in before and after-NFT DAUF test, and "sum incorrect" even decreased in after-NFT DAUF test. Besides, other 3 subjects all got improved performance in DAUF test, either by increased sum correct or decreased sum incorrect, which supports the efficiency of NFT. The paired t-test was applied to sum correct, mean time correct, sum incorrect, and mean time incorrect of before and after NFT shooting sessions separately, however, no significant difference was found.

4.3   Correlation Analysis

In this section, we further studied the correlation between the change in shooting performance and in DAUF test. We subtracted the before NFT shooting score/DAUF results from the after NFT shooting score/DAUF results and then calculated the correlation coefficients using the changes of NFT shooting score and DAUF results. We expect a positive correlation between the change of shooting scores and of DAUF test results.

Table 6. DAUF test results before and after NFT.

Subject ID	DAUF test results	Session ID	
		S1	S2
1	Sum correct	279	252
	Mean time correct	0.701	0.829
	Sum incorrect	4	4
	Mean time incorrect	0.682	0.898
2	Sum correct	264	271
	Mean time correct	0.749	0.756
	Sum incorrect	6	9
	Mean time incorrect	1.002	0.718
3	Sum correct	278	278
	Mean time correct	0.6	0.615
	Sum incorrect	4	3
	Mean time incorrect	0.61	0.636
4	Sum correct	273	275
	Mean time correct	0.556	0.572
	Sum incorrect	5	4
	Mean time incorrect	0.438	0.578
5	Sum correct	279	279
	Mean time correct	0.784	0.765
	Sum incorrect	4	2
	Mean time incorrect	0.846	0.738

Due to limited number of subjects, we could not get significant correlation. However, the trend of correlation is compatible with our hypothesis as presented in Table 7. The change of total shooting score is positively correlated with sum correct, and negatively correlated with mean time correct, sum incorrect, and mean time incorrect, which indicates that the improvement of shooting score between before and after-NFT session is accompanied with the increase of sum of correct reaction in DAUF test, decrease of mean reaction time for correct reaction, sum of incorrect reaction, and mean reaction time for incorrect reaction.

Table 7. Correlation study.

Correlation coefficients	Sum correct	Mean time correct	Sum incorrect	Mean time incorrect
Total score	0.41	−0.7	−0.205	−0.6

4.4   Brain States Before and After-NFT

We also compared correlation between shooting scores and the brain pattern right before the shot release in before and after NFT shooting sessions. Well-established EEG power features such as alpha, beta, theta, and beta/theta ratio were used to analyze the brain pattern. Initially, 2 out of 5 subjects had negatively correlated shooting scores against beta power whereas after NFT all 5 subjects exhibited positive correlation. The change may indicate that the subjects were able to adjust their brain pattern by the NFT. It is consistent with the literature [17] which stated that gymnasts and athletes were able to improve attention and emotional stability after NFT. Apart from the change in beta band in the after NFT shooting sessions, higher alpha is associated with better performance as it indicates more relaxed brain state [41]. This is also in line with our results where NFT has resulted in a positive correlation between alpha band power and shooting performance for 4 out of 5 subjects.

Additionally, the effect of NFT was analyzed by study of the asymmetric brain pattern. Two channels were used to get the difference of brain activity between left and right hemisphere. The results showed that before NFT, the difference of SMR band (12–15 Hz) was positively correlated with the shooting score for 1 subject in parietal lobe whereas after NFT all 5 subjects had positive correlation. Similarly, the difference of beta was positively correlated with shooting performance for 2 subjects when parietal lobe channels were used in the before NFT shooting session. However, we could see beta was positively correlated with shooting performance for 4 subjects in the after NFT shooting sessions. Besides, we found that before NFT, 3 out of 5 subjects had positively correlated beta/theta ratio with shooting score. For different EEG bands, 3 out of 5 had positive correlation with theta and 2 out of 5 had positive correlation with both beta and alpha. After NFT, 3 out of 5 subjects had positively correlated ratio values. All 5 subjects had positive correlation with theta and beta, and 4 out of 5 subjects had positive correlation with alpha.

We further extended our study to compare the correlation between brain states such as mental workload and emotion, and shooting performance in before and after NFT sessions using the workload/emotion recognition algorithms introduced in Sect. 1.

We found out that in the shooting sessions before NFT, only 2 out of 5 subjects had negative correlation between the average workload for 4 s before the trigger of the shot and shooting scores. The negative correlation means that lower mental workload (i.e. lower mental efforts) of the shooter before the shot release is associated with the better shooting score. As a contrast, in the shooting sessions after NFT, the average mental workload for 4 s before the trigger of the shot is negatively correlated with the shooting performance for 4 out of 5 subjects. The difference of mental workload states before shot release in the before and after NFT session could be because of NFT. The change of emotional state after NFT is not as obvious as workload. By analyzing the average emotion, mental workload and power features for all the 40 shots in each session, it could be seen that 2 out of 5 subjects had either more positive or neutral emotion after NFT. Also, 2 subjects had lower mental workload after NFT. Before NFT, 3 out of 5 subjects had neutral emotion and 4 out of 5 subjects had medium or low workload. After the NFT, 4 out of 5 subjects' emotion were either positive or neutral and 3 out of 5 subjects had lower or moderate level of workload.

5   Conclusion

In this paper, we proposed a novel NFT protocol based on individual beta/theta ratio to improve cognitive abilities of rifle shooters. We designed and conducted an experiment with five elite rifle shooters who participated in up to 7 NFT sessions. We showed that the NFT could help the shooters boost the performance as the shooters had improvement in the after NFT shooting session and sustained attention test DAUF. We also showed that a positive correlation exists between the change of shooting scores and of DAUF test results. By attending NFT sessions, the shooters were able to adjust their brain states which can be seen from the correlation changes between EEG band power, workload/emotions and the shooting performance in the before and after NFT sessions.

Limited number of elite shooters was recruited to participate in the project experiments because of their tight schedule. Statistical significance was not obtained in the data analysis but the results are consistent with the literature review. In the next step, we expect to recruit more shooters in the study.

Acknowledgement. This research is supported by the National Research Foundation, Prime Minister's Office, Singapore under its International Research Centres in Singapore Funding Initiative. We would like to acknowledge the final year project students of School of EEE of Nanyang Technological University and personally Jessica Kathryn Liddon for her contribution in this work.

References

1. Burke, L.M., Gollan, R.A., Read, R.S.: Dietary intakes and food use of croups of elite Australian male athletes. Int. J. Sport Nutr. **1**(4), 378–394 (1991)
2. Maughan, R., Shirreffs, S.: Development of hydration strategies to optimize performance for athletes in high-intensity sports and in sports with repeated intense efforts. Scand. J. Med. Sci. Sports **20**(s2), 59–69 (2010)
3. Laursen, P.B.: Training for intense exercise performance: high-intensity or high-volume training? Scand. J. Med. Sci. Sports **20**(s2), 1–10 (2010)
4. Laursen, P.B., et al.: Interval training program optimization in highly trained endurance cyclists. Med. Sci. Sports Exerc. **34**(11), 1801–1807 (2002)
5. Hibbs, A.E., et al.: Optimizing performance by improving core stability and core strength. Sports Med. **38**(12), 995–1008 (2008)
6. Birrer, D., Röthlin, P., Morgan, G.: Mindfulness to enhance athletic performance: theoretical considerations and possible impact mechanisms. Mindfulness **3**(3), 235–246 (2012)
7. Mamassis, G., Doganis, G.: The effects of a mental training program on juniors pre-competitive anxiety, self-confidence, and tennis performance. J. Appl. Sport Psychol. **16**(2), 118–137 (2004)
8. Liu, Y., et al.: Neurofeedback training for rifle shooters to improve cognitive ability. In: 2017 International Conference on Cyberworlds (2017)
9. Liu, Y., Sourina, O.: Real-time subject-dependent EEG-based emotion recognition algorithm. In: Gavrilova, M.L., Tan, C.J.K., Mao, X., Hong, L. (eds.) Transactions on Computational Science XXIII. LNCS, vol. 8490, pp. 199–223. Springer, Heidelberg (2014). https://doi.org/10.1007/978-3-662-43790-2_11

10. Lim, W.L., et al.: EEG-based mental workload recognition related to multitasking. In: Proceeding of the International Conference on Information, Communications and Signal Processing (ICICS) (2015)

11. Sanei, S., Chambers, J.A.: Brain rhythms. In: EEG Signal Processing, pp. 10–13. Wiley, Cardiff (2007)

12. Becerra, J., et al.: Neurofeedback in healthy elderly human subjects with electroencephalographic risk for cognitive disorder. J. Alzheimer's Dis. **28**(2), 357–367 (2012)

13. Lubar, J.F.: Neurofeedback for the management of attention-deficit/hyperactivity disorders. In: Biofeedback: A Practitioner's Guide, 2nd edn., pp. 493–522. Guilford Press, New York (1995)

14. Clarke, A.R., et al.: Electroencephalogram differences in two subtypes of attention-deficit/hyperactivity disorder. Psychophysiology **38**(2), 212–221 (2001)

15. Egner, T., Gruzelier, J.H.: EEG biofeedback of low beta band components: frequency-specific effects on variables of attention and event-related brain potentials. Clin. Neurophysiol. Off. J. Int. Fed. Clin. Neurophysiol. **115**(1), 131–139 (2004)

16. Rostami, R., et al.: The effects of neurofeedback on the improvement of rifle shooters' performance. J. Neurother. **16**(4), 264–269 (2012)

17. Liu, Y., Hou, X., Sourina, O., Bazanova, O.: Individual theta/beta based algorithm for neurofeedback games to improve cognitive abilities. In: Gavrilova, M.L., Tan, C.J.K., Iglesias, A., Shinya, M., Galvez, A., Sourin, A. (eds.) Transactions on Computational Science XXVI. LNCS, vol. 9550, pp. 57–73. Springer, Heidelberg (2016). https://doi.org/10.1007/978-3-662-49247-5_4

18. Di Fronso, S., et al.: Neural markers of performance states in an Olympic athlete: an EEG case study in air-pistol shooting. J. Sports Sci. Med. **15**(2), 214 (2016)

19. Kim, W., et al.: A comparison of cortico-cortical communication during air-pistol shooting in elite disabled and non-disabled shooters. Pers. Individ. Differ. **54**(8), 946–950 (2013)

20. Wang, Y., Huang, T.: Effects of neurofeedback training on EEG and pistol shooting performance. In: Conference for Chinese Society of Sport Psychology, Wuhan, China (2006)

21. Kerick, S.E., Douglass, L.W., Hatfield, B.D.: Cerebral cortical adaptations associated with visuomotor practice. Med. Sci. Sports Exerc. **36**(1), 118–129 (2004)

22. Mikicin, M.: The autotelic involvement of attention induced by EEG neurofeedback training improves the performance of an athlete's mind. Biomed. Hum. Kinet. **7**(1), 58–65 (2015)

23. Paul, M., Ganesan, S., Sandhu, J.S.: Effect of sensory motor rhythm neurofeedback on psycho-physiological, electro-encephalographic measures and performance of archery players. Ibnosina J. Med. Biomed. Sci. **4**(2), 32–39 (2011)

24. Babiloni, C., et al.: Golf putt outcomes are predicted by sensorimotor cerebral EEG rhythms. J. Physiol. **586**(1), 131–139 (2008)

25. Ring, C., et al.: Investigating the efficacy of neurofeedback training for expediting expertise and excellence in sport. Psychol. Sport Exerc. **16**, 118–127 (2015)

26. Nan, W., et al.: Beta/Theta neurofeedback training effects in physical balance of healthy people. In: Jaffray, D.A. (ed.) World Congress on Medical Physics and Biomedical Engineering. IPMBE, vol. 51, pp. 1213–1216. Springer, Cham (2015). https://doi.org/10.1007/978-3-319-19387-8_294

27. Arns, M., Conners, C.K., Kraemer, H.C.: A decade of EEG theta/beta ratio research in ADHD: a meta-analysis. J. Atten. Disord. **17**(5), 374–383 (2013)

28. Hamadicharef, B., et al.: Learning EEG-based spectral-spatial patterns for attention level measurement. In: IEEE International Symposium on Circuits and Systems, ISCAS 2009. IEEE (2009)

29. Gevensleben, H., et al.: Distinct EEG effects related to neurofeedback training in children with ADHD: a randomized controlled trial. Int. J. Psychophysiol. **74**(2), 149–157 (2009)

30. Bazanova, O., Aftanas, L.: Individual EEG alpha activity analysis for enhancement neurofeedback efficiency: two case studies. J. Neurother. **14**(3), 244–253 (2010)
31. Liu, Y., Sourina, O., Hou, X.: Neurofeedback games to improve cognitive abilities. In: 2014 International Conference on Cyberworlds (CW) (2014)
32. ViennaTest. http://www.schuhfried.com/viennatestsystem10/vienna-test-system-vts/
33. Emotiv. http://www.emotiv.com
34. Bazanova, O., Aftanas, L.: Individual measures of electroencephalogram alpha activity and non-verbal creativity. Neurosci. Behav. Physiol. **38**(3), 227–235 (2008)
35. Turin, A., Johnson, W.G.: Biofeedback therapy for migraine headaches. Arch. Gen. Psychiatry **33**(4), 517–519 (1976)
36. Fumoto, M., et al.: Appearance of high-frequency alpha band with disappearance of low-frequency alpha band in EEG is produced during voluntary abdominal breathing in an eyes-closed condition. Neurosci. Res. **50**(3), 307–317 (2004)
37. Lehrer, P.M., Vaschillo, E., Vaschillo, B.: Resonant frequency biofeedback training to increase cardiac variability: rationale and manual for training. Appl. Psychophysiol. Biofeedback **25**(3), 177–191 (2000)
38. Caldwell, J.A., Prazinko, B., Caldwell, J.L.: Body posture affects electroencephalographic activity and psychomotor vigilance task performance in sleep-deprived subjects. Clin. Neurophysiol. **114**(1), 23–31 (2003)
39. Bazanova, O., Vernon, D.: Interpreting EEG alpha activity. Neurosci. Biobehav. Rev. (2013)
40. Vernon, D., et al.: Alpha neurofeedback training for performance enhancement: reviewing the methodology. J. Neurother. **13**(4), 214–227 (2009)
41. Hoedlmoser, K., et al.: Preparatory EEG spectral power and coherence in biathlon rifle shooting: a pilot study. In: 3rd International Congress on Science and Nordic Skiing (2015)

Author Index

Ang, Hock Eng   15
Antony, Palesa   29

Beuck, Sandra   1
Braun, Melinda C.   1

Chua, Joshua   106

Fushimi, Shota   90

Gatzidis, Christos   57
Gavrilova, Marina   75

Harihara Subramaniam,
    Salem Chandrasekaran   15, 106

Ivanov, Kirill   106

Konovessis, Dimitrios   15
Krishnan, Gopala   15

Liew, Serene Hui Ping   15
Lim, Wei Lun   15
Liu, Yisi   15, 106

Mangoale, Bokang   29
Mao, Xiaoyang   90
Masango, Mfundo   29
Mouton, Francois   29

Pedersen, Karsten   57

Roeling, Mark Patrick   43

Scheurer, Alexander   1
Shah, Eesha   106
Silomon, Jantje A. M.   43
Sourina, Olga   15, 106

Tang, Wen   57
Toyoura, Masahiro   90

Wang, Lipo   15
Wölfel, Matthias   1

Xu, Caie   90
Xu, Jiayi   90

Zohra, Fatema Tuz   75

Printed in the United States
By Bookmasters